Y0-EMC-159

COLLEGE OF MARIN LIBRARY
COLLEGE AVENUE
KENTFIELD, CA 94904

YES Means YES, Everything Else Means NO

Bruce Mullen

Copyright © 2023

All Rights Reserved

Dedication

To my incredible son, Brandon, and my lovely daughter, Caitlyn,

We've gone through thick and thin together, and I couldn't be prouder of the incredible individuals you're becoming. Every day, as I watch you both grow, I'm filled with great optimism.

You, my dear children, are destined to leave a long-lasting mark on this world, not just with the beauty of your lives but with the kindness and impact you bestow upon others.

May your paths be filled with adventure, learning, and the courage to carve your own path, just as I've tried to impart in this book. Always remember, your potential is boundless, and your hearts—pure gold.

With all my love and the utmost faith in your bright futures,

Dad

Acknowledgment

This book, *"Yes Means Yes. Everything Else Means No,"* has been a journey of discovery, growth, and learning, much like life itself. I want to extend my heartfelt gratitude to those who've contributed to this endeavor, directly or indirectly, knowingly or unknowingly.

First and foremost, to my family for being my pillars of support. To my older brother, Murray, who unknowingly inspired the core principle of this book, and to my children, Brandon and Caitlyn, who continually remind me of the significance of leading by example.

To the countless people who shared their stories and experiences, both uplifting and challenging, thank you for showing me the many shades of life. Your experiences, like the diverse notes in a symphony, have added depth and richness to the narrative.

I'm profoundly grateful for the many mentors, teachers, and guides whose wisdom has shaped my understanding. To the countless authors, thinkers, and innovators whose work influenced the ideas within these pages, thank you for your contributions to the world of knowledge.

To my readers, thank you for investing your time and trust in the words written here. Your quest for wisdom and your pursuit of personal growth inspires me.

Lastly, to life itself, for its unending capacity to teach and transform. Your lessons are ceaseless, sometimes challenging, but always invaluable.

This book reflects the collective wisdom of those who've walked beside me on the road to transformation. Let's cherish life's beautiful complexities and the endless potential it offers.

With deep appreciation and a heart full of gratitude,

Bruce Mullen

Table of Contents

About the Author

You could call Bruce a true Canadian trailblazer. He dedicated his entire career to Mullen, a company that's not just on the Toronto Stock Exchange but has become a powerhouse under the name Mullen Group (MTL).

Working side by side with his father, three brothers, and a dedicated team of employees, friends, and shareholders, Bruce helped transform Mullen into one of Canada's giants in transportation, logistics, and energy services.

But Bruce's influence extended far beyond the boardroom. He served on the Board of Directors for companies like Producers Oilfield Service and Horizon Logistics, contributing his expertise to their success.

Safety has always been at the heart of Bruce's mission. He chaired the Upstream Petroleum Industry Task Force On Safety (UPITFOS), ensuring the well-being of those working in the energy sector. As a member of the Board of the Petroleum Service Association of Canada (PSAC), his commitment to safety was monumental.

Bruce's dedication reached even the most remote corners of Canada. He implemented safety programs and procedures across aboriginal committees in Northern Alberta, British Columbia, and the far reaches of the Northwest Territories.

His efforts didn't go unnoticed. Bruce received recognition from the Energy Industry Rotary Club of Canada for his unswerving commitment to safety and his relentless pursuit of enhanced operational procedures.

But Bruce's journey didn't stop in the "energy business." Today, he's channeling his boundless energy into something equally powerful—the "human energy" business.

As the Founder of Jusu Bars, Inc., he's taking his passion for well-being and safety to a whole new level.

In every chapter of his life, Bruce has shown a remarkable dedication to making things better, safer, and more efficient. He's a visionary, and his story is far from over.

Preface

Welcome, dear reader, to *"Yes Means Yes. Everything Else Means No."* I'm delighted to present my book to you. This book is a culmination of life's lessons, experiences, and reflections. Its purpose is simple yet weighty: to explore the art of mindful living, leadership, and self-discovery.

But why this book?

The birth of these pages was a chance encounter with a phrase that became my guiding light: *"Yes means yes. Everything else means no."* It was a wisdom passed down by my older brother, Murray, and over the years, it's become a personal mantra, a life philosophy, and a compass directing my choices.

This book is designed to take you through a thought-provoking and illuminating journey, much like a thrilling adventure. Together, we'll delve into the concept of living life deliberately, valuing the spirit of leadership, learning from our mistakes, and building trust in all aspects of our lives.

We'll also explore the art of seizing the moment, being present, and learning as we go. Each chapter presents a unique facet of this philosophy, connecting the dots between real-life experiences and the remarkable wisdom contained within these pages.

You'll find here no promises of overnight success, no magical shortcuts to the pinnacle of achievement. Instead, these pages are a companion, a source of inspiration, and a gentle nudge to challenge your perceptions, contemplate your choices, and steer your own course.

It's not a preachy sermon; it's a chat among friends. It's an invitation to reflect, learn, and grow together.

I encourage you to read on, not as a passive consumer of words but as an active participant in your own discovery. Consider how these ideas resonate with your life, your choices, and your aspirations. Relate them to your own experiences, and write your story as you go.

Chapter 1

Yes Means Yes, Everything Else Means No

"Yes means yes. Everything else means no."

What the hell does that mean?

Well, let me tell you, my friend, this simple phrase has become my guiding principle in life. It's my compass, my North Star, my secret weapon. And today, I want to share its incredible power with you.

It all started with my older brother, Murray. He was a no-nonsense kind of guy, always saying, "Clear written requirements. That's how you know what needs to be done correctly." I admired his straightforward approach, but I wanted to take it a step further and simplify it even more. That's when it hit me: "Yes means yes. Everything else means no."

Let me break it down for you. Have you ever asked someone how they're doing, and they replied with a vague "fine" or "all right"?

Well, what they really meant was "no." Let me explain how. In business, when you're working on a contract, and someone says, "Great," when asked if they have a contract ready to sign, you might as well take it as a no. Yes is focused, precise, and direct, while no has a wide, wide scope. These are the lessons that I have learned.

My brother, Kevin, once told me about an employee who left his company and left a note on his desk, saying, "One of the most important things I've learned here is yes means yes. Everything else means no." This young woman had learned a valuable lesson about clear communication, and it changed her life for the better.

Now, let's apply this powerful principle to various aspects of life. In personal relationships, it can be a game-changer. If your date says, "I'll give you a callback," after you ask to meet again, guess what? That's a no. If your partner responds to your dinner suggestion with an indifferent, "Oh, that sounds okay," that's a subtle no.

Remember, clarity is key.

In business, this principle is equally valuable. When your boss says, "I'm looking into it," after you ask for a raise, that's a no. And when you ask your kids if they've done their homework and they reply with an optimistic "Almost done," well, you guessed it—that's a no, too.

But it doesn't stop there. Yes means yes. Everything else means no applies to how we deal with the world around us. It's about reading people and understanding their personalities. You see, there are different types of individuals out there, each with a distinct personality type.

The ABCD Personality Types were the brainchild of cardiologists Meyer Friedman and Ray Rosenman back in the swinging '50s.

Originally, it was all about Type A and Type B, but the concept expanded to include the intriguing Type C and enigmatic Type D personalities.

These personalities serve as a sort of map, guiding us through the complexity of behaviors, attitudes, and stress responses that make each of us gloriously unique.

Type A Personality

Imagine the epitome of ambition, competition, and a dash of impatience. These individuals are like turbo-charged engines, always striving for the top spot and expecting nothing less than perfection. They set the bar high, not just for themselves but for everyone around them. While this drive may lead them to professional triumphs, it may be tricky, too. The Type A's intense work ethic can also stir up a storm of stress, potentially opening the door to health concerns like hypertension and heart disease. So, while these go-getters may conquer the corporate jungle, they must also learn to dance in the rain.

Type B Personality

Picture a serene garden on a sunny day—relaxed, easy-going, and content. These folks have mastered the art of enjoying the journey, cherishing every moment along the way. They're creative, imaginative souls who know how to savor life's simple pleasures. Unlike their Type A counterparts, they don't lose sleep over every little detail or mistake. While they may not have the same frenetic pace, their approach often leads to a smoother ride and lower stress levels. They're the maestros of "going with the flow," navigating life's twists and turns with a smile on their faces.

Now, let's meet the **Type C Personality**, the analytical wizards.

Think meticulous attention to detail, logical thinking, and an unrelenting pursuit of precision. These individuals thrive on structure, logic, and the thrill of diving deep into data. They're the architects of order in a world that sometimes seems chaotic. However, with great precision comes a unique challenge—emotional stress. Yes, the Type C's analytical prowess may inadvertently lead them into the clutches of emotional turmoil. That's right, buried beneath all those well-organized spreadsheets and impeccably crafted plans lies a sea of emotions waiting to be explored.

Lastly, we encounter the enigmatic **Type D Personality**— the empathetic explorer of emotions. These compassionate souls are in tune with their own feelings and those of others. They're the friends who always lend a listening ear, the healers who embrace the human experience with open arms. Type D personalities are often introverted, deeply introspective, and skilled at understanding the human psyche. Yet, this emotional sensitivity can be a double-edged sword. While they possess the gift of empathy, they may also experience chronic emotional stress, wrestling with the waves of worry and negativity.

The thing is, these personality types are not rigid boxes. Instead, they are unique expressions of a person's psyche that create the masterpiece of our individuality. And just as our preferences for ice cream flavors evolve over time, so too can our personality traits shift and grow.

So, now the question arises, what's the point of all this?

Well, let me paint you a picture.

Imagine finding the perfect job that aligns with your strengths and work style—a career that fuels your passion and ignites your drive. Imagine forging relationships that are meaningful and fulfilling, built on a foundation of mutual understanding. Imagine working on your personal growth, shedding old habits, and embracing new perspectives.

These personality types are a tool to decode the complex dance of human interaction. Armed with this knowledge, you can craft a life that resonates with your core, managing stress like a seasoned Jedi and harnessing the power of your unique traits.

As you navigate the intricacies of this complex world, it's crucial to remind yourself to keep things simple. Take a deep breath, clear your head, and consciously block out the noise.

But what do I mean by "noise"?

Noise is that intrusive voice in your head—the self-doubt and self-criticism that tells you that you aren't good enough. It's that nagging feeling that drags you down and makes you question your choices and abilities. It can be the internal chatter that undermines your confidence and prevents you from taking bold steps forward. You need to get your facts sorted first.

But noise isn't just limited to your internal thoughts; it can also manifest externally. External noise can come in the form of people who don't root for you or support your dreams. These individuals might go out of their way to make you feel insecure or try to undermine your progress.

Be vigilant and watch out for such people. They can be disguised as friends, acquaintances, or even colleagues. They may feel threatened by your potential for success or simply enjoy seeing you doubt yourself. Surrounding yourself with negativity can be toxic, and it's essential to distance yourself from those who hinder your growth and well-being.

Remember, it's okay to create boundaries and protect yourself from harmful influences. Surround yourself with people who uplift and inspire you, those who genuinely want to see you thrive and succeed. Seek out a support system of individuals who believe in your capabilities and are there to cheer you on in both good times and bad.

"If you surround yourself with idiots, you will become an idiot. If you surround yourself with great people and friends, you will for sure be a better person."

You are in charge of your life, and simplicity will help you make better decisions, prioritize things well, ask better questions, and get clearer answers.

But let's be honest; keeping things simple isn't always easy. It's tempting to get tangled up in other people's dramas, but remember, you can't control what others think of you. Focus on understanding them instead.

Communication is vital in this process. Listen more than you talk. My brother always said, "If you talk enough, you'll say something dumb."

Wise words, I must admit, it's true.

So, work on your communication skills, understand different personalities, and build better relationships with those around you.

I've got three core components to share with you that form the foundation of any flourishing connection:

Mutual Respect

When you're in a healthy relationship, you both hold each other in high regard. It's like having your own personal fan club! You admire each other's qualities and the beautiful character traits you both possess.

Mutual Trust

Trust-the glue that keeps it all together. In a healthy relationship, you take each other at your word. If someone says they'll do something, you bet your sweet honey they'll follow through. Trust means being honest, even when it's uncomfortable. It's like having a truth serum on hand at all times.

Mutual Affection

In a healthy relationship, affection flows freely and is received with open arms (or maybe hugs). There's no need to remind yourself to show love and appreciation; it comes naturally. And if physical contact and intimacy are important, you both engage enthusiastically—though, let's be real, nobody's always "in the mood."

Now, remember, love is the fantastic product of a healthy relationship—not the foundation for it. Crazy, right? But true. You can love someone deeply, even if they're absolutely terrible for you (been there, done that).

Love alone isn't enough to sustain a relationship. Instead, true, unconditional love blossoms when two people create a healthy bond with each other. You must put in maximum effort, especially when you doubt each other.

Now, what happens when the core components of a healthy relationship start to erode?

Well, it's like a house of cards—the whole thing can come tumbling down. Lose affection, and trust can crumble. Lose trust and respect might follow suit. It's a tricky balance, my friends.

3 steps forward, 2 steps back.

Nothing goes straight up. Go back and get common ground.

Just as it can spiral downward, it can spiral right back up! If you find yourself or your partner going through a transformation, you might lose some respect for each other. That's okay—it happens. What's important is finding new sources of respect in your relationship and embracing the change.

Now, if mistakes are made (and we all make them), trust might take a hit. But fret not! Give it some time, make sure it's a one-time thing, and be open to forgiveness. We're all human, and minor mistakes are usually a breeze to overcome. It's the bigger ones that require more TLC.

Remember, not every relationship is smooth sailing. But with a little effort and understanding, a toxic relationship can transform into a healthy and thriving one.

Now, let's talk about productivity. A conversation that must be had.

Imagine that you're a highly motivated individual, always seeking productivity hacks and ways to optimize your work. You dive headfirst into new apps, try out morning rituals, and experiment with various time management techniques. This is where my "blocking out the noise" advice comes in handy.

However, in this pursuit of productivity, you might find yourself getting burnt out, overwhelmed, and losing sight of what truly matters.

I've been there too, my friend. That's why I shifted my focus away from the latest productivity trends and instead delved into understanding my own psychology. After all, productivity is a deeply personal thing, and what works for one person might not work for another. We all have unique brains, preferences, perspectives, and situations where we feel most effective.

Procrastination, for instance, is deeply connected to anxiety. To tackle it effectively, it's crucial to develop a deep understanding of your own neuroses and fears.

Be open to self-awareness, and you'll find that action gains momentum. Personal rituals that kickstart your productivity are far more valuable than the fanciest apps or yoga routines.

Every morning, as the sun begins to rise, I find a serene spot in my home, a cozy corner near the window with a breathtaking view of the world awakening. I take a few moments to appreciate the beauty of the new day, soak in the energy of the rising sun, and connect with nature.

With a steaming cup of my favorite coffee in hand, I sit down comfortably and open my journal—a trusted companion that holds my thoughts, dreams, and aspirations. This journal is more than just a record of events; it's a canvas for my innermost reflections. My friends, family, and loved ones.

I begin my personal ritual with gratitude. I list three things I am grateful for from the previous day—simple joys, small victories, or moments of connection with loved ones. This practice grounds me and reminds me of the blessings in my life, no matter how big or small.

I think about my kids if they are happy. I know I am onto a great start.

Next, I rummage into self-awareness. I take a moment to check in with myself, examine my emotions, and identify any thoughts or feelings that might be holding me back. This process of self-reflection allows me to confront any doubts or insecurities that might be lingering in the depths of my mind.

Then, I set my intentions for the day ahead. I outline my top three priorities—the tasks or goals that will make the most significant impact on my work and personal growth. I focus on these key objectives to ensure that I channel my energy and efforts toward what truly matters.

Before I move on to tackle the day's challenges, I engage in a short visualization exercise. I close my eyes and imagine myself successfully completing each of my priorities. I visualize the sense of accomplishment and fulfillment that comes with achieving my goals. This visualization ignites a fire within me and thrusts me into action.

I decide if it is *"a good day or a struggle."*

With my intentions set and my vision clear, I take a final moment to reaffirm my self-belief. I repeat a positive affirmation—a mantra that I've crafted for myself to reinforce my confidence and determination. This affirmation reminds me that I am capable, resilient, and worthy of success.

I try to look into the future and gain a broader perspective.

Now, I'm ready to face the day. Armed with gratitude, self-awareness, clear intentions, and unwavering self-belief, I step into the world with a renewed sense of purpose. The personal ritual I've carved out helps me cut through the noise, stay focused, and prioritize my time and energy on what truly matters.

And here's the beauty of it all: this ritual is about the simple act of connecting with myself, understanding my inner world, and aligning my actions with my values and goals. Through this daily practice, I find that action gains momentum, and I am empowered to seize each day with enthusiasm and purpose.

Remember, positive is always better.

In the creative process, I discovered that work doesn't always follow a linear function. The misconception that the more hours you input, the more productive output you create can lead to frustration and burnout.

While some basic, repetitive tasks exhibit linear returns, most thoughtful, brain-intensive work does not. It's essential to recognize that your brain tires out, and its ability to effectively be productive diminishes over time.

Most days, I found that my best work came in the first 1-2 hours. Beyond that, the returns were mixed, and after a certain point, my productivity and ideas took a nosedive. It was as if my creativity had a limited fuel tank, and pushing it beyond its capacity only resulted in more work to clean up the mess I had created.

Work that requires problem-solving and critical thinking follows a curve of diminishing or even negative returns. You might try to push yourself to work longer hours, but there comes a point where your efficiency starts to decline, and the quality of your output suffers. Just like a muscle that gets tired, your brain also needs rest and rejuvenation to stay sharp.

You must learn to power down.

Recognizing leverage points in your work is vital. Focus on aspects that have a multiplier effect on everything else. A ritual to boost team morale, new skills for problem-solving, or improve your branding can elevate your overall productivity. On the other hand, deleverage points slow down your progress, hindering your effectiveness. Eliminate the noise and focus on the top three things on your to-do list. Deem everything else as noise.

Don't fall into the trap of *"the religion of hustle."* Working longer hours doesn't always translate to greater productivity. Instead, strategic procrastination—a well-deserved break from intense problem-solving can recharge your mind and make you even more effective upon returning to work.

That's when the concept of working smarter, not harder, became crystal clear. Instead of forcing myself to work longer hours, I began to recognize the importance of strategic breaks and rest in the creative process. Taking a step back, allowing my brain to recharge, and returning with a fresh perspective led to bursts of creative brilliance.

You see, creativity flourishes in an environment of balance—a delicate blend of intense focus and rejuvenation. Strategic procrastination is not laziness; it's a well-deserved break from intense problem-solving, allowing your mind to process and connect the dots subconsciously.

Just as you need a variety of foods to stay healthy, your mind craves diverse stimulation to stay sharp. Embrace leisure time, weekends, and vacations as opportunities for your brain to recharge and reset. It's not laziness—it's a smart strategy for long-term productivity and happiness.

The "say yes until you have to say no" principle is a powerful strategy that works wonders in various aspects of life. Early in your career, it's crucial to seize every opportunity that comes your way.

Even if some seem peculiar, irrelevant, or inconvenient, embrace them with a resounding "yes." You never know which doors they might open and what valuable experiences they can provide.

As you grow and your skills and reputation start to shine, you'll find yourself drowning in a sea of opportunities. It's at this point that you must strategically wield the power of "no."

Saying "no" allows you to focus your efforts on the opportunities with the most significant potential and propel yourself further, faster. You find yourself becoming more selective. You'll even reach a stage where you have to decline almost every opportunity that comes your way—a true mark of success.

This principle is not just limited to business but permeates into every aspect of life:

- If you move to a new city and seek to make friends, accept every invitation until you become so popular that you can start turning down the lamer parties.

- If you're single and on the hunt for a meaningful relationship, meet everyone until you find those special people worthy of a "no" to those with terrible Tinder profiles.

- If you're on a journey of self-discovery, say yes to trying everything until you're forced to say no. Ultimately, you'll uncover what truly matters to you.

Mastering the skills of saying both "yes" and "no" is essential, yet it's something few people naturally excel at simultaneously.

For some, saying "yes" comes effortlessly, but they struggle to say "no." These people-pleasers find themselves entangled in a busy social life and abundant career opportunities.

However, their inability to let go of what's unimportant and their fear of disappointing others might leave them feeling "trapped" in a life they never chose or desired.

On the other hand, there are those who find it difficult to say "yes." They are contrarians and loners who pride themselves on spotting and avoiding deception. While this can make them feel smart and superior, their hesitance to fully commit prevents them from building something they can truly be proud of. These individuals might be perceived as hipsters and has-beens.

Striking a balance is key—the secret sauce lies in knowing when and how to use both "yes" and "no."

Avoid being worn down in the long run by saying "yes" indiscriminately. Similarly, don't miss out on valuable opportunities by always saying "no." Understanding the art of saying (and hearing) both "yes" and "no" will empower you to navigate life with wisdom and confidence.

"Yes means yes, everything else means no" is more than just a catchy phrase—it's a life-changing principle. Harness the power of simplicity and clear communication in your personal and professional relationships. Understand that love alone isn't enough to sustain a relationship; it's the result of a healthy bond built on mutual respect, trust, and affection.

When it comes to productivity, remember that it's not about working longer hours but working smarter. Recognize the leverage points in your work and the diminishing returns of prolonged problem-solving. Give your brain the rest and variety it needs to stay sharp and effective.

The "say yes until you have to say no" principle is your ticket to unlocking endless opportunities. Welcome every experience, even if it seems odd or inconvenient, as it might lead to unexpected doors opening in your life. As you grow and evolve, strategically start saying "no" to focus on the opportunities that truly matter.

Remember, saying both "yes" and "no" is an art to master. Don't fall into the trap of people-pleasing or contrarianism. Instead, strike a balance by knowing when and how to use both affirmatives and negatives.

So, my friends, go forth and embrace the magic of "Yes means yes. Everything else means no." Let this principle guide you to a life of clarity, purpose, and fulfillment. You have the ability to shape your destiny, and with this guiding principle, you can make every moment count.

May you find the strength to say "yes" to the right opportunities and confidently say "no" when needed!

Chapter 2

Getting Started

The wise Aristotle once mused, "We are what we repeatedly do. Excellence, then, is not an act but a habit." In this chapter, I will teach you how to master your mornings, where the seeds of triumph await.

Have you ever noticed that when your morning begins in a whirlwind of chaos like snoozing alarms, skipping breakfast, and rushing out the door—the rest of your day seems to mirror that frenzied state?

The morning, my friends, is the foundation upon which the tone of your day is built. Hence, it is high time to craft your morning rituals with thoughtful intention.

Getting started is also setting your foundation for how you will live your life.

It is critical to start your day right.

Our lives are woven with habits, whether we acknowledge them or not—both the virtuous and the not—so—virtuous ones. To develop healthy habits, we must embrace intentionality. Often, habits form because they're easy or simply along the path of least resistance. But if we seek to nurture positive habits, we must consciously put effort into embedding them until they become second nature. And this holds especially true for our morning rituals.

What transpires in the early hours influences how we feel, act, and think throughout the entire day. And so, I present to you some simple habits to integrate into your morning routine to pave the way for a day and days of boundless potential.

Firstly, resist the temptation of checking your smartphone immediately upon waking. Welcome present-moment awareness by detaching from technology for that first sacred hour of the day. It's an empowering shift from reactive to proactive thinking, developing inner peace and control.

Next, welcome the refreshing embrace of a hot beverage—a revitalizing elixir to awaken your body.

Before even leaving the warmth of your bed, grant yourself a moment to smile and express gratitude. This act not only releases those delightful feel-good neurotransmitters but also nurtures a sense of contentment.

Then, the simple yet impactful act of making your bed. This seemingly trivial task actually cultivates a sense of accomplishment—a foundational stepping stone to tackle greater challenges ahead.

Now, let us commune with our inner selves through meditation—an invaluable practice to ground our minds and emotions. Set intentions for the day during this peaceful rendezvous, and you'll find yourself making clearer decisions to craft the life you truly desire.

Momentum gathers as we partake in some morning movement. Be it a gentle yoga session, a brisk walk, or a quick workout, this energizing practice ignites both the body and mind, setting a vibrant tone for the day.

Taking care of your appearance isn't just about vanity; it contributes to self-confidence. So, shower, groom, and dress in a way that makes you feel fabulous.

Break your fast with a nourishing breakfast—lean proteins, healthy fats, and whole grains—the fuel that sustains your energy levels and sharpens your focus.

Map your day's journey with a purposeful "to-do" list. Keep it concise and prioritize tasks, for clarity of goals empowers you to make the most of each moment.

And let us not forget the crux of it all—restful sleep. Quality slumber fuels our physical and mental well-being, making it essential for a vibrant day ahead.

Breathe and move your body—be it yoga, walking, or a swift workout—motion invokes vitality.

Pen your goals for the day, savor a moment of quietude, and say hello to a loved one to spread positive energy. Learn the art of saying "no" when needed and reap the benefits of a well-rested body and mind.

As you set forth, remember to visualize your day's achievements powered by the upbeat rhythm of the music. Treat yourself to some downtime, for it aligns your focus and fuels a centered mind.

The way you start your morning sets the tone for the entire day, so make it a good one. It's not just about checking off a list of tasks like a *"Real Adult";* it's about setting yourself up for success by prioritizing your mental and physical well-being. Every morning, your brain's willpower reserves are at their highest, but they're not limitless. As the day goes on, decision fatigue sets in, making it harder to resist instant gratification.

A good morning routine can be the key to conserving your willpower and making better decisions throughout the day.

When you automate your mornings with healthy habits, you free up your mind to focus on more important decisions later on. Plus, many morning activities can serve as acts of self-care on their own.

Remember, a morning routine is not about squeezing in as many tasks as possible but creating a sustainable and mindful practice that supports your well-being and helps you navigate the day with intention.

Stoic Wisdom

"When you first rise in the morning, tell yourself: I will encounter busybodies, ingrates, egomaniacs, liars, the jealous, and cranks. They are all stricken with these afflictions because they don't know the difference between good and evil."

— *Marcus Aurelius*

Stoicism, a profound branch of philosophy, offers a practical and robust framework for those of us treading the complexities of the real world. It aims to cultivate resilience, happiness, virtue, and wisdom, ultimately leading to personal growth and betterment in various aspects of life.

Throughout history, Stoicism has left its mark on great leaders, spanning from Marcus Aurelius to Theodore Roosevelt and beyond. Emperors, writers, thinkers, and entrepreneurs have all been influenced by its timeless teachings. The preserved writings of these remarkable individuals, including private diaries, personal letters, and lectures, provide us with a wealth of wisdom that still resonates with us today.

Amidst the noise and distractions of modern life, finding inner tranquility is absolutely vital. The ancient philosophy of Stoicism offers valuable tools for cultivating these qualities and leading a harmonious life. It can be a powerful philosophy for setting the tone for the day, as it offers practical principles and techniques to create balance in your routine.

Embracing the Virtues

Stoicism centers around the four cardinal virtues — wisdom, courage, justice, and temperance. You can reflect on these virtues in the morning and establish a moral compass to guide your actions and decisions throughout the day. This helps set the tone for a day driven by ethical principles, self-discipline, and fairness.

Practicing Gratitude

Stoics encourage a gratitude practice to start the day. When you acknowledge the blessings in your life and express appreciation, you can attain a positive and contented mindset. This gratitude practice helps you focus on abundance and joy rather than dwelling on what may be lacking.

Negative Visualization

Engaging in negative visualization in the morning can prepare you to face potential challenges with equanimity. When you imagine worst-case scenarios and mentally prepare for adversity, you develop resilience and maintain inner peace when confronted with difficulties. This is how you can work on your composure and adaptability.

Journaling

Journaling in the morning allows individuals to articulate their intentions, emotions, and reflections. This simple act helps you grow a sense of self-awareness and self-improvement. By putting thoughts into writing, you can reinforce your commitment to virtuous living and remind yourselves of your guiding philosophy throughout the day.

Focusing on What's Within Your Control

One of the fundamental teachings of Stoicism is the dichotomy of control — distinguishing between what is within our power and what is not. When you acknowledge and accept what cannot be changed, you can focus your energy on what you can influence. This helps develop a proactive and constructive approach to challenges.

Cultivating Mindfulness

You must emphasize the importance of living in the present moment and practicing mindfulness. When you are fully present in each task and interaction, you can savor the richness of the present and reduce distractions. This helps you inculcate in yourselves a sense of groundedness and purpose.

Seeking Inner Freedom

Stoics believe that true freedom lies in mastering one's emotions and desires rather than being controlled by external circumstances. When you find inner freedom, you can emotionally detach from unnecessary attachments.

Accepting Impermanence

Stoicism reminds us of the impermanence of life and the transitory nature of things. Building on this perspective, you can develop a sense of detachment from fleeting highs and lows, replenishing your day with equanimity and a steady outlook.

Secrets To a Happy Life

Happiness is a unicorn that every person dreams of catching. Can we ever really be truly content with our lives? The answer lies in the effort you are willing to put into the pursuit. Let me share some concepts that will help you get started:

#1: Beliefs

First and foremost, you must understand that beliefs are deeply personal and unique to each individual. We all hold our own set of beliefs, which may or may not align with any particular religion. The key is to acknowledge that everyone has their own beliefs and to approach others with an open mind and curiosity.

Asking questions is the most powerful tool to understand and strengthen our beliefs. When we seek information and understanding, we can avoid unnecessary conflicts and uplift ourselves and others.

#2: Thoughts

Research has shown time and again that our thoughts have a profound impact on our mindset and actions. Positive thoughts lead to positive actions and, in turn, build positive lives. Jay Shetty, a monk-turned-life coach, introduces the "Spot, Stop, Swap" technique to address negative thought patterns effectively.

Spotting negative thoughts allows us to become aware of their presence. Once we catch ourselves having these negative thoughts, we can stop and reflect on whether they serve us or not. If not, it's time to swap them out for more positive and true thoughts. It's not about pretending everything is perfect but rather finding genuine, empowering thoughts that lead to better outcomes.

#3: Words

Communication is key to strong relationships, and that includes using diverse vocabulary to express our emotions accurately. Instead of settling for basic descriptions like "I'm sad," we must expand our emotional vocabulary.

When we explore and communicate our feelings more precisely, we gain intimacy and understanding in our relationships.

#4: Actions

Our actions play a crucial role in shaping our lives, and forming positive habits is the key to success. Changing your actions requires breaking them down into small, manageable steps.

Rather than attempting drastic changes overnight, focus on making gradual adjustments that build positive habits. Small, consistent steps can lead to significant transformations over time.

#5: Intentions

Finally, we must realize the power of our intentions. The intention to bring value and happiness to others can lead to a more fulfilling life for ourselves as well.

When we align our beliefs, thoughts, words, actions, and intentions with compassion, kindness, and mindfulness, our energy becomes uplifting to those around us. This synergy brings us happiness, success, and inner peace.

The Power of Positivity

Positive thinking is not a magical solution to all of life's challenges, but it is a mindset that focuses on the good and expects positive outcomes. It's about anticipating happiness, health, and success instead of dwelling on negative possibilities.

However, it's essential to acknowledge that positive thinking alone isn't enough to realize your dreams.

Here are six ways you can harness the power of positive thinking and transform your entire mindset.

#1: Empower Yourself

Take responsibility for your thoughts, actions, and emotions. Align with an internal locus of control, understanding that you have the power to change yourself and your reactions to events. When you empower yourself, you build a deep belief in your abilities, generating a positive mindset that can withstand failures and setbacks.

#2: Take Control of Your State

Your physiology and body language are closely linked to your mindset. Take pride in how you present yourself, stand tall, make eye contact, and exude confidence. This positive body language not only affects how others perceive you but also reinforces a positive mindset within yourself.

#3: Adjust Your Mindset

Your mindset determines how you interpret and react to events. Train yourself to focus on positive moments and reframe negative thoughts. Develop an abundance mindset that is grateful and open rather than one that dwells on negativity and limitations.

#4: Study Your Habits and Form New Ones

Be aware of negative habits and defense mechanisms that hold you back. When you catch yourself in a negative thought pattern, consciously replace it with positive affirmations. When you train your mind to block negativity with positive thoughts, you'll gradually shift your mindset towards positivity.

#5: Choose Your Words Carefully

Transform your vocabulary to include more positive language. Be mindful of how you label and describe situations and emotions. Replace negative words with positive alternatives to promote a positive mindset in yourself and those around you.

#6: Identify Those You Admire

Seek inspiration from individuals who have made positive thinking their mantra to achieve remarkable success. Mentors, role models, or quotes from respected figures can provide valuable reminders and encouragement to maintain a positive mindset.

Remember, the power of positive thinking goes hand in hand with taking action and overcoming limiting beliefs.

The Nike Principle

Motivation isn't just the passenger of the motivation train; it's also the powerful engine that sets it in motion. We often wait for that emotional spark to ignite before taking action toward our goals. You know, like hitting the books when we're terrified of failing the exam or strumming that guitar when we're inspired by the music we want to create for others.

But, my friend, here's the twist in the plot: sometimes, negative emotions play a sneaky role in holding us back from the actions we need to take. Imagine wanting to fix a strained relationship with your mother, but emotions like hurt and resentment prevent you from taking the necessary steps, like having an honest conversation.

So, how do we break free from this paradox and get the motivation to train back on track? Introducing the legendary *"Nike Principle."* This genius technique is your secret weapon to ignite motivation in your life.

You see, action, inspiration, and motivation are all part of a never-ending loop. When you take the tiniest action, even the most mundane task, it sparks a chain reaction. Suddenly, you find yourself inspired and motivated to do more and more! It's like a snowball effect of positive momentum.

This principle will work wonders for you. Building my business, I faced moments of doubt and uncertainty. Oh, the temptation of TV reruns and comfy couches! But, I learned that if I pushed myself to do even the smallest task, like designing my company logo, it would lead me down a delightful rabbit hole of productivity.

It's all about taking incentive, starting somewhere, taking action, no matter how tiny, and using it to unlock your motivation and inspiration. The "Nike Principle" is your trusty sidekick on the epic journey toward your goals! Remember to just do it! And you will watch yourself climbing every mountain and overcoming every roadblock with finesse.

Enduring Discomfort

Living consciously, my friend, is no walk in the park. It takes effort, determination, and a dash of courage. Each time we choose to raise our consciousness, we take a stand against inertia—the tendency of everything to descend into chaos. We strive to create a haven of order and clarity within ourselves.

But let's face it: we all have our foes to conquer. Laziness, which may be the manifestation of inertia and entropy in our minds, is one of them. We've all experienced those moments when we fail ourselves simply because we couldn't muster the effort for an appropriate response.

And then there's that other pesky monster—the impulse to avoid discomfort. Embracing conscious living might mean confronting fears and facing unresolved pain. It could even shake our "official" self-concept. But let me tell you, this journey to self-acceptance and self-responsibility is worth it. When we dare to be authentic, embrace self-assertiveness, and choose our values, we open the door to a life filled with purpose and integrity.

Now, let's talk about the ultimate treasure awaiting those who tread these trepid waters—self-esteem and happiness. High self-esteem individuals, believe it or not, are happier folks. But here's the thing: building self-esteem requires us to endure some discomfort along the way.

It's true that avoiding discomfort isn't inherently wrong, but if it blinds us to important realities and leads us away from necessary actions, it becomes a tragic roadblock. We must break free from the cycle of avoidance, where each layer of disowned pain piles on top of another.

But fear not! There is a path to victory over these challenges. It starts with a simple decision—to prioritize our self-esteem and happiness over short-term pain. Taking baby steps towards consciousness and self-acceptance, we notice a delightful transformation. As we grow, so does our self-esteem, making it easier to confront uncomfortable emotions and situations.

Don't get me wrong; it won't be a stroll in the garden. Effort and courage are essential companions on this journey. Yet, as we persevere, we build our spiritual muscles, and we become more resilient in the face of fear and pain.

The key is to recognize that this process doesn't have to be overwhelming. We can give a gentle nod to fear and discomfort as natural aspects of life and face them with grace, moving steadily towards our best possibilities.

So, remember that the love we have for our own life is the fuel that propels us forward. It's the seed of virtue, and it launches us toward our highest aspirations.

Chapter 3

Mistakes Happen

We all share a common companion — mistakes.

Yes, those inevitable missteps that often leave us cringing in the spotlight of our own imperfection. But let's take a moment to unravel the truth: mistakes are not malevolent forces conspiring against us. Instead, they are part of our genetic code, creating a plethora of experiences that shape us into the fascinating beings we are today.

Imagine this: if life were a grand recipe, mistakes would be the secret ingredient that gives it that extra kick. You see, regret is like staring at a puzzle piece you can't seem to fit anywhere. It's uncomfortable, frustrating even. But here's the twist: it's meant to be that way. Regret isn't a harsh critique of who you are; it's an invitation to explore the intricacies of your journey.

So, why does regret sometimes feel like a relentless raincloud?

Well, let's unravel the layers.

When you make a mistake, it's like hitting an unexpected fork in the road. Your past self took a certain path, and now, you're here. But rather than beat yourself up over the "wrong" turn, what if you embrace that former self? Picture having a conversation with them, unraveling the intentions and motivations that led to that choice.

Think of it as a heart-to-heart with your past. It's about understanding, not chastising. Maybe that past version of you was navigating uncharted waters, relying on the tools they had at that moment.

You're a product of all those accumulated moments.

You can empathize with your past self. That way, you're offering yourself a dose of compassion, like a soothing balm for the wounds of regret.

Now, let's talk about the difference between a mistake and its cousin, regret. Mistakes are like rough sketches, waiting for the artist's touch to refine and perfect them.

A regret, however, is a masterpiece waiting to be unveiled, its true meaning tucked beneath the surface. It's like looking at a puzzle and realizing that each piece, no matter how awkwardly shaped, contributes to the bigger picture.

Imagine if Edison had lamented every failed attempt at the light bulb. We'd still be living in the dark. Learning from mistakes, my friend, is like discovering a treasure map to personal growth. When you glean insights from your missteps, you're not just avoiding future blunders – you're polishing your own potential.

Here's a tip: Regret can be your ally, not your adversary. It can serve as a compass, guiding you away from rocky shores toward calmer waters. It's all about perspective, turning "I messed up" into "I learned and grew."

Remember, a flower doesn't bloom without enduring a little rain.

And speaking of perspective, let's zoom out for a moment. Our narratives tend to be myopic, centered around the present, and heavily influenced by emotions. But let's sprinkle a dash of wisdom here: setbacks can be the launchpad for comebacks.

That financial mishap you endured?

It might have been the cosmic nudge you needed to reassess your values and priorities.

That painful heartbreak?

It could have been the catalyst for your emotional growth, paving the way for deeper connections.

Don't let your narrative be the villain. Embrace the long game. A mistake today can be the victory of tomorrow. After all, the most potent antidote to regret is a narrative that spans years, woven with threads of growth and transformation.

Now, let's address the fear of failure. Imagine life as a playground and failure as your exuberant playmate. When you engage with failure, you're not just playing tag; you're engaging in a dance of discovery.

Failure isn't a one-way ticket to disappointment—vile. It's your gateway to character development. It's through these moments that you learn to pivot, adapt, and thrive. Failure is your ticket to the VIP lounge of growth.

Let's circle back to our primal instincts. Our ancestors feared mistakes because they meant life or death.

But in the modern world, the stakes have shifted. A typo in an email won't summon a saber-toothed tiger. Yet, our brain's primitive wiring can still send the "danger" signal. It's time to rewire that circuit.

Mistakes are the breadcrumbs leading you to innovation.

If things aren't failing, you're not innovating enough.

So, if you find yourself in the embrace of failure, take a bow. You're on the cutting edge of progress.

And let's not forget the art of learning from mistakes. Think of it as building a repertoire of strategies. You're amassing a toolbox that's brimming with wisdom, ready to tackle whatever life throws your way.

Remember, it's not the stumble that defines you; it's the grace with which you rise.

When a mistake knocks on your door, don't slam it shut. Invite it in, offer it a seat. Engage in a dialogue, for within those moments of vulnerability lie the seeds of transformation.

So, when you stumble, when you fumble, when you take that detour you didn't plan for, remember this: you're not lost.

You're simply adding another chapter to your epic tale.

The Plane Crash

I've got a story to share, a story about a colossal mistake – the biggest one I've ever been a part of. It was a heart-stopping plane crash, and right there with me was my daughter Caitlyn.

Let me take you back to June 28, 2021. So much of my life revolves around what unfolded on that day. You see, I became a pilot some three decades ago, soaring over Western Canada and the western United States, from the Mexican border to the Arctic Ocean. I've touched down on gravel strips, grass strips, major airports, tiny ones – you name it. I've racked up well over 3,000 hours of being the boss in the pilot's seat.

Planes?

Oh, I've owned a trio of single-engine beauties. First came the trusty Cessna 182 retractable gear, then the '81 Beechcraft Bonanza, and later, the sleek 2009 Beechcraft Bonanza G36. And let me tell you, I'm no slouch in the certification department. I've got my private pilot's license, a knight rating, and even a mountain rating. I've trained with American Airlines pilots, been to Bonanza school, and wrestled with flight simulators. Yeah, I've had my fair share of intense training.

Now, I'm not one to tiptoe through the clouds. I prefer to keep things grounded, using flight following like a trusty co-pilot. It's a bit like rubbing shoulders with the major airlines, always keeping an eye on where I am.

Now, brace yourselves because this tale takes a grim turn when I send my beloved plane in for the annual maintenance ritual. You know, that thorough checkup to keep everything spick and span, which, by the way, needs to be reported to the bigwigs at Transport Canada.

During this routine maintenance, a phone call sent a shiver down my spine. It was about one of the cylinders, apparently running low on compression. The maintenance company – the ones I'd trusted since the dawn of my plane's existence – offered two options: fix it up over the span of a month or get a spanking—new assembly and be on my way. I opted for the new one, trusting that these folks knew their nuts and bolts.

Eventually, the plane was declared ready for action, all polished and prepped, sitting there waiting for me in the hangar. Excitement bubbled up – my daughter Caitlyn and I were embarking on a quick flight back home to the Sunshine Coast in North Vancouver, a mere 20-minute jaunt. The plan was to put that annual maintenance behind us, but oh, what a twist of fate awaited.

Before we took to the skies, I performed the preflight ritual like a seasoned conductor. Logbook? Check. Signatures? Double check. The walk-around got extra attention, especially with Caitlyn on board. Lift-off from Victoria was smooth as silk, and we cruised over to the Sechelt Airport, ticking off procedures left and right. Heck, we even had a 20-minute tête-à-tête with air traffic control. Our landing was spot-on, and the plane was snugly tucked away. I was on cloud nine.

But then reality hit like a lightning bolt. An email from the maintenance company disrupted the serene post-flight glow. A hefty $20,000 bill stared back at me, a stark reminder that life can hand you turbulence even on the clearest days.

I've always had one rule – no shortcuts. It's a mantra I've lived by, a safeguard against risks. The thing is, risks have a way of sneaking up on you, even on seemingly perfect days.

It was a clear, hot day, a light aircraft, a well-maintained machine, and my daughter by my side. We were all set for a smooth ride, heading over the ocean on the West Coast. With life jackets strapped, seatbelts secure, and everything in perfect working order, we took off. We climbed to a comfortable 4500 feet above the coast, with plenty of altitudes to spare.

Then, chaos descended. The Garmin 1000's once calm display turned into a frenzy of red warnings. The number two cylinder went rogue, knocking and vibrating like a madman. Panic took hold, but I kept my cool. Tightened seatbelts, and I called a MAYDAY out to Victoria Tower as I sought a safe spot to land amidst the trees and rugged terrain of the West Coast.

The scene turned surreal – a desperate dance against time and odds. The plane shuddered violently, and the computer screamed as we fought gravity's grip. A terrifying plunge, a roar of engines tearing free, and we crashed into the trees. Yet, somehow, the passenger door remained level with the ground, Caitlyn's lifeline to safety. With urgency in my voice, I guided her out, and fate sent an ICU nurse, our guardian angel, to whisk her away from the looming danger.

The crash scene was chaos, with sirens blaring and first responders racing against time. The clock ticked, and flames threatened, but their expert hands worked miracles. The fire was quenched, and I was pulled from the wreckage just as the flames licked at my heels. A hazy blur of pain and fear followed, and I awoke in an ICU bed, a new chapter of survival unfolding.

Caitlyn, too, faced a battle, with surgeries, scans, and medications becoming her companions. As the days and nights merged, all I could think was: I almost lost my daughter. It was a never-ending nightmare, a 24/7 ordeal on the path to recovery.

And me? I'm learning to walk again, pushing through the pain with therapy and determination because a great day can be a struggle on its own.

The facts are that the wrong cylinder was installed in my plane engine. The failure of the maintenance company, the Engine manufacturer distributor, the Engine manufacturer, plus Transport Canada caused this engine failure. But somehow, we survived!

Now, let me lay it out straight – mistakes happen, even to those who pride themselves on caution. And you know what I learned the hard way? It's not enough. It's not enough to assume the checks are done, the i's dotted, and the t's crossed.

Here's the deal: you've got to be your own advocate. You've got to ensure your maintenance company is playing by the rules, following the policies and procedures. Don't take shortcuts when it comes to the safety of your loved ones. And remember, having insurance isn't a golden ticket. You've got to check if they're covered from nose to tail, just like you do.

The truth is, the engine company, the ones who should care, often don't. Once that check clears, it's as if they wash their hands of it. I mean, really? A simple cross-reference of serial numbers should be a no-brainer, right? Yet, in this convoluted system, it's often overlooked.

So, let me drop this truth bomb: flying is a privilege, a dance with the skies that demands respect. It's not something to take lightly because when things go south, they can do so in a heartbeat. And I'm here to tell you, that's when the hindsight hits harder than the impact.

Now, I'm not an aviation expert, just a pilot who's had to navigate the storm. I'm not saying you should be petrified, but you should be vigilant. When you board a small plane, feel comfortable asking questions, and here are some helpful ones for your pilot:

1. **Is your pilot's license up-to-date?**
2. **What's the scope of your insurance?**
3. **When was the last inspection, and is it insurance-approved?**
4. **Ensure we're not overloaded with excessive weight.**
5. **Make a thoughtful choice about your travel plans!**

My dad always said, *"You have to have a lot of money if you keep making the same mistakes over and over again."*

It's a good lesson.

Risk Management

This is the kind of lesson that life hammers into you until it becomes your unwavering mantra. Manage your risks, whether it's in your health, at home, on the road, or even when you're chasing dreams in the workplace or having fun.

Trust me, I've been through the wringer on this one, and while I can't lay claim to a monopoly on making mistakes, I sure as heck have learned from them. And let me tell you, the lessons I've learned the hard way aren't the ones you'll soon forget.

You know, there's a guy named Robert McNamara who was tapped by President Kennedy to work his magic as the Secretary of Defense back in the early 60s. But before that, he was the big cheese over at Ford Motor Company. Now, under McNamara's watch, Ford took a leap of genius by putting seatbelts in their 1957 Falcon.

A wild idea, right? The thinking was that if you package people up snugly and properly in vehicles, there'd be fewer things breaking, especially humans.

Turns out, getting folks to buckle up wasn't exactly a cakewalk. But the ones who did? They lived to tell the tale. It's a classic example of how it took time for people to wise up about seatbelts and even car seats for the little ones. You see, the name of the game here is risk reduction, and the lessons can sometimes be written in tragedy.

Ever tried convincing someone that prevention is the key to making fewer mistakes?

Trust me, you can burn through more oxygen on that one than a marathon runner.

Now, let me take you on a ride through the trucking, oilfield, and logistics business that I was knee-deep in, along with my dad and brothers.

Every single day, every shipment, every task, one simple mantra – *"nobody gets hurt, nothing gets damaged."*

Oh, and getting paid that's a pretty crucial part of the equation, too.

We've clocked hundreds of millions of miles and moved tens of thousands of loads from itty-bitty jobs to massive ones.

But you know what our ultimate goal was?

To ensure not a single person got hurt and nothing, absolutely nothing, got banged up.

Why?

Well, it's not just because we're the good guys – it's also because it's just good for business.

Our recipe for success?

Well, for starters, we believed in a level playing field at work. Quality equipment? You bet. We made sure our gear was tip-top and up to snuff. And education? Oh boy, that was non-negotiable. We trained ourselves and our team day in and day out. No slacking.

Accidents happen. Yeah, they're not a result of some cosmic coincidence. It's usually because the policies and procedures, the ones put in place to save our hides, just aren't followed.

Now, back in my early days, way before we called it the fossil fuel business, it was the "oil patch."

Hardhats? Steel-toed boots? Reflective coveralls? Pssh, those were luxuries.

We'd just dive in, get the job done, and if things got wrecked or someone got hurt, well, that was just part of the game.

But you know what?

We thought that was downright wrong.

So we went ahead and turned things around. Hard hats became as essential as air, steel-toed boots were like a second skin, and those funny reflective vests? Yeah, they became a non-negotiable part of the uniform. Of course, there was some grumbling, but hey, we put our money where our mouth was.

And we didn't just stop there. We partnered with oil companies, making safety our top priority. And plenty of them saw the light. They started hopping on the safety train, and the industry, well, it started evolving.

I was even part of an industry task force focused on safety and transportation. We pioneered certification programs in the oil field, with a sweet bonus of demerits shaving off your driving record if you completed the course. We decked out coveralls with reflective stripes, making vests practically obsolete.

And the payoff? Fewer accidents, fewer mistakes.

The bottom line, my friends, is that it all boils down to training, education, commitment, and always striving for top-notch performance. You don't just pull out the big guns when you feel like it. Oh no, you keep your game face on all the time.

So, when you glance around a job site today and see folks sporting hard hats, steel-toed boots, ear protection, eye protection, and reflective gear, and you know they've been trained up, take a moment to appreciate it.

These improvements aren't just cosmetic. They're the result of learning from mistakes, sometimes ones that came at a painful cost.

"No means try harder."

There is a name for the fear of messing up and making mistakes: atelophobia.

Trust me, it's not a term you want to be on a first-name basis with.

Now, let's get one thing straight from the get-go – everyone, and I mean everyone, makes mistakes. It's like a universal truth, right up there with gravity and the fact that pizza is the greatest invention ever.

So, how you deal with those blunders, how you wrangle those mishaps, can actually shape your entire existence.

Let's say you've got this nagging feeling that you might mess things up, so what do you do?

You start avoiding certain situations like the plague, or maybe you constantly find yourself lagging behind, putting things off, or even dodging social gatherings where you might just end up sounding like a clueless goof.

But why the heck are we so petrified of making mistakes in the first place?

Well, the answer is seemingly variable. Maybe you're terrified that one tiny slip-up could send your career or reputation swirling down the drain. Or perhaps you've set the bar impossibly high for yourself, and the mere thought of your flaws being laid bare has you breaking into a cold sweat. If any of this rings a bell, you might just be hanging out with our friend Atelophobia.

Now, atelophobia isn't just a quirky term to throw around at dinner parties – it's a real thing, and it can throw a serious wrench into your life. Imagine being stuck in a never-ending loop of self-judgment and criticism, where you feel like you're constantly falling short of your own sky-high expectations.

So, what do we do about the mistakes we make?

Mistakes, my friends, are the unsung heroes of life.

No, really! Think about it: all those missteps, blunders, and facepalms are the stepping stones to some serious wisdom.

See, perfectionism's like that overly ambitious cousin who never shows up to the family BBQ; it's just not realistic, and it takes the joy out of the whole dang experience.

But the beauty is when you stumble and fall, you're not just failing. You're learning. And that's a one-way ticket to enlightenment and growth. You know all those things you've been itching to learn but never had the guts because you were petrified of messing up?

Yeah, think about learning a new language, learning a new dance move, tackling a marathon, or even just mending fences with someone you've had a beef with. These are lessons to be learned.

Atelophobia might just be the GPS you never knew you had. You see, a lot of us are cruising through life on autopilot, unaware that there's this little voice called atelophobia guiding our decisions and steering us away from risky business. It's like having a backseat driver who's hell-bent on keeping you in the safe lane. But once you face that fear head-on and realize it's just a bunch of smoke and mirrors, you become the master of your own journey.

People will judge you and try to bring you down. That's a given. You can't let someone else's idea of perfection dictate your actions. Drop that list of criticisms playing on repeat in your head, take a deep breath, and be brave.

I want you to appreciate your blunders, make friends with your failures, and dance with your mistakes.

Because at the end of the day, it's those very missteps that carve out the path to your success. Take the time to manage risks in all your endeavors – in your career, your relationships, and your personal pursuits.

Chapter 4

Trust

The Real Currency of Life

Trust is like a puzzle piece that fits perfectly in a relationship. If you get it right, it's seamless, but if you lose it, it's like losing a piece of the puzzle – impossible to restore.

So, what does trust really mean?

According to the trusty dictionary, it's about having that rock-solid belief in the reliability, truth, strength, or ability of someone or something.

That sounds like a no-brainer, right?

But let's be real – it's a tougher nut to crack than you'd think. It's easier to catch a cloud in your hand than to get trust and way simpler to see it slip through your fingers.

You can slap a price tag on your car, your house, your favorite pair of sneakers – pretty much anything you can touch or see. But trust? Nope, that's not something you can buy with all the gold in the world. Once trust takes a nosedive, it's like a sandcastle swept away by the tide – no amount of "I'm sorry" can rebuild it.

Trust is a commitment. It's a pact with yourself.

You know that colleague you side-eye during meetings? Yeah, we've all got one. You might not trust them entirely, but you still gotta get the job done together. Think of it as working with a caution sign hanging over your head. Trust, my friends, it's like slipping on your coziest socks – it just makes life that much more comfortable.

But let's take a detour into the facts – trust isn't just for sealing business deals. It's like the holy grail for your personal life, the kind that keeps you sane when the world goes haywire. When *"show me, don't tell me"* becomes your mantra, that's when trust steps into the spotlight. It's not just words; it's a whole lifestyle. It's how you rise and shine every morning and how you lay your head down at night, knowing you've done right by yourself and others.

Ever noticed how trust is thrown around like confetti these days?

People talk about trust as much as they talk about the weather. But beware, not everyone's a truth-teller. We've got "trust me" slogans on 24-hour news channels, where they promise the moon and deliver... well, something that's not quite the moon. In a world where "alternative facts" have become a thing, it's the real trust that's your North Star – in relationships, in business, and in life itself.

Let me tell you, I've spent my entire career on a trust-building mission. It's not just about clients; it's about everyone – colleagues, stakeholders, even the barista who hands me my morning brew. Treating everyone with respect is the cornerstone. You see, I've got role models in my life – my parents. If trust was a sport, they'd be Olympic champions. They've built their lives around hard work, integrity, and leading not by holding hands but by setting examples that light the way.

Now, let's talk legacy – my parents have etched trust into our family's DNA. Their lesson isn't just about balancing checkbooks; it's about balancing values and integrity. They're 89 and 92, still kicking and teaching us that life isn't all sunshine and rainbows, but a strong foundation of trust can weather any storm.

So, how do you build trust?

Building trust isn't a weekend project. It's a skyscraper you construct brick by brick. It's about choosing the right actions over easy words, about walking the talk when everyone else is just talking.

It's not some popularity contest where everyone votes on who's the most likable. Trust is a 24/7 commitment, a lifestyle. Life's gonna throw you curveballs – personally and professionally. Brace yourselves, 'cause not everyone's gonna be clapping for your decisions. If your goal is to make everyone happy, you're in for one wild rollercoaster ride.

And hey, if you're ever caught in a situation where someone's not happy with your decisions, remember my dad's wise words: "They'll either get over it or they won't."

And let's cut the jargon – the basics of trust boil down to honesty, integrity, and perseverance. Don't overcomplicate it; it's the ABCs of life.

Now, I'm not losing sleep over what folks think of me. But you know what keeps me up? Trust. Yeah, I might sound tough as nails, but I've learned this: if I lose sleep over every person who doesn't like my choices, I'd be starring in a sleep-deprived horror movie.

So, let's break it down. Stay focused. Look in the mirror every morning and remind yourself you're giving it your all. That's good enough. You can't catch Zs when you're on a mission to please everyone. Some can juggle that circus act, but I'm not in that ring. My focus? If you can trust me.

Let's talk tough stuff – saying "sorry" won't stitch the trust fabric back together. Nope, actions speak louder than that word ever could. Trust is a delicate bird; once it flies away, you can't just call it back. It's like watching a golf channel – yeah, I know, it sounds weird. My wife asks me why I watch that golf channel so much. But it's that one place on TV where the volume is as soothing as a lullaby, the kind that puts you right to sleep. It's my meditation, my zen.

Speaking of golf, Tom Lehman had a golden nugget about the future. He said it's pretty simple: you need someone to love, something to do, and a dash of hope for the future. Now, that's a life recipe.

Here's a truth bomb – people are watching your moves, not your lip service. Actions write the script, my friends. I chat with people day in and day out and trust me, what I think I'm saying isn't always what they hear.

Oh, and remember Robert McNamara?

He was spot-on – answer the question you want, not the one you got, especially when you're in the dark. Making stuff up? That's a trust crusher. Like I said, my brother always said if you talk enough, you'll say something dumb.

Flip on the news, and you'll see it – words flowing like a river. But the real tale is told by actions. We're here for a reason, a simple one. We're here to fuel ourselves and our loved ones. Being healthy, yeah, that's a must. But it's not just about smoothies; it's about fueling trust, too. Your body and your relationships – they need that good stuff.

"Don't Underestimate Momentum "

Our business thrived not 'cause everyone loved us but because people trusted us. Sure, not everyone was cheering, but we held on. So, let's wrap it up with this: look in that mirror, remind yourself that you're giving it your all, and let the sunrise greet you with a fresh start. Trust me, the world is better with a little more trust in it.

Let's get real about this – a lot of personal relationships crumble because trust goes AWOL.

And let me tell you, that sting? It's like a punch in the gut.

Sure, people can be forgiving, but push them too far, and guess what?

You're gonna see if they've got integrity in their DNA if they've got the backbone to weather the storm if they've got that fierce desire to live their best lives.

You must learn the art of trust-building, and here are some savvy strategies to get you started:

Walk the Talk

If you want folks to buy what you're selling (metaphorically, of course), you've gotta be consistent in your words and actions. Don't be a promise-maker who forgets to follow through. It's like promising a surprise party and delivering a wet blanket instead – not cool. And no, it's not just about keeping your word but also about not throwing around promises you can't keep. That's a trust sinkhole you don't want to be in.

Craft the Perfect Communication Recipe

Poor communication stands for relationship disaster. Trust me, no one likes playing a game of "Guess What's on My Mind." So, why not serve up clear, concise, and honest communication instead? Make sure you're on the same page. There is no room for misunderstandings. And remember, communication isn't just talking. It's about being an A-list listener, too. Be that person who understands, not the one who zones out mid-conversation.

Patience, My Friend, Patience

Quick wins are great for lotteries but not so much for trust-building. Rome wasn't built in a day, and neither is trust. Start with small commitments and work your way up. Trust isn't a sprint; it's a marathon. Plant the seeds of trust, water them with consistency, and let time work its magic. Believe me, the harvest will be worth it.

Think Before You Leap

Ever heard the phrase *"measure twice, cut once"*? Well, the same goes for trust. Think before you make commitments. Saying yes and then backtracking is like starting a puzzle and then tossing away a piece – it messes up the whole picture. Be honest about your plate's fullness and only bite what you can chew. Staying organized is like the GPS for trust-building.

Cherish the Bonds

Remember that friend who's always got your back through thick and thin? Yeah, that's the trust goldmine. Relationships flourish when consistency is the name of the game. Be there, rain or shine. Trust me, your presence matters. And respect is like the crown jewel in the trust kingdom. Never belittle or condescend – respect builds trust, and disrespect tears it down.

Embrace Your Team Spirit

Life is a team sport, my friend. Show up and give you're a-game. Engage, contribute, and let your team skills shine. When you're part of the trust-building squad, you're all about reciprocity. Show them you trust them, too, and it's like a trust domino effect.

The Honesty Pact

Honesty is the superstar of trust-building. No sugar-coating, no white lies. Keep it real, even if it's a tough pill to swallow. A lie, no matter how small, chips away at trust. So, let's not play that game. When you're the truth-teller, your trust stock shoots through the roof.

Spread the Kindness Vibe

Helping others isn't just good karma; it's a trust-building masterstroke. Authentic kindness is the answer. Extend a hand without expecting anything in return, and you'll see trust blossoming like spring flowers. It's like a magic spell, trust me.

Don't Lock Away Your Emotions

Be an open book, not a locked diary. Emotions on display are like the neon sign of trust. Show that you care, and watch your trust meter start soaring. Embrace emotional intelligence – it's like the secret ingredient to trust smoothies.

It's Not All About You

Shoutout to the self-promotion squad – dial it back a notch. Acknowledge others, appreciate their efforts, and you'll earn the trust gold star. Trust isn't a solo journey; it's a duet. And ditch selfishness because it is trust's arch-enemy.

Trust Your Inner Compass

Doing what's right isn't just about following the herd. It's about sticking to your values and beliefs. Yes, sometimes it might ruffle feathers, but trust me, authenticity trumps conformity. Trust is like a truth serum; it reveals who's real and who's just saying what sounds good.

Own Up to Oops Moments

Hey, we're all human. Mistakes happen. But you must admit them. Hiding your mishaps is a trust buster. Vulnerability is the path to trust, showing you're not a flawless robot. When you're open about your stumbles, trust grows stronger.

Minding Relationships

Ever heard of *"minding"* in relationships? It's like the superglue that keeps bonds strong. It is equal doses of empathy, companionship, and commitment, all mixed up in a recipe for relationship success. It's about sharing, attributing, and accepting – the ultimate trust-building combo.

Share Your True Colors

Remember when you were a kid and could spot a fib from miles away? Yeah, that skill's still with you. So, if you say you'll do something, do it. And don't play the promise game if you're not up for it. Trust me, being reliable is the key to a solid foundation.

Get Cozy with Vulnerability

Want to level up the trust game?

Be open, be real. Vulnerability is your secret weapon. Show your softer side, admit your fears, and let your partner see the real you. Trust is like a dance – sometimes you lead, sometimes you follow, but you're always in sync.

Respect: The Trust Keystone

Respect – it's like trust's VIP pass. Disrespect, it's the trust-killer. Whether it's a casual chat or a deep conversation, treat your partner with respect. Think of it as the golden rule of trust-building – do unto others as you'd have them do unto you.

Let's talk about why trust is so important to relationships, especially in the workplace. Whether you're a team member or the big boss, trust is your VIP ticket to a world of benefits you won't want to miss out on.

The Dream Team Formula

Imagine your workplace as a bustling beehive. When trust is buzzing around, your team functions like a well-oiled machine.

Distrust, on the other hand, is like throwing a wrench into that machine. Team members might hold back their insights or ideas, fearing someone will snag them for personal gain. Trust sparks a symphony of shared knowledge, while distrust creates a solo act.

Boosted Morale, Tamed Stress

In a trust-rich atmosphere, you're breathing in the freshest workplace air. It's because you're not busy glancing over your shoulder, worried someone's going to pull a fast one on you. Less stress equals more productivity. When trust is the foundation, stress is like a deflated balloon, and productivity soars to new heights.

The Productivity Power-Up

Meet the productivity destroyer: untrustworthy colleagues. They're like productivity black holes, sucking up energy and resources with their antics. Gossip and lack of cooperation run rampant, and the work rhythm goes out of tune. In a trust-filled environment, productivity thrives. Even saving just 10 minutes a day from unproductive activities per employee can make a massive impact on the company's bottom line.

Change Becomes a High-Five Moment

Change is as constant as your morning coffee – especially at work. But change can be a fear-fueled roller coaster if trust isn't in the picture. In a trusted sanctuary, change is greeted with curiosity, not fear. When trust is like an old friend, resistance and anxiety vanish, making change a thrilling adventure rather than a dreaded ordeal.

Employee Performance

Imagine your supervisor as your trust mentor. When trust is mutual, feedback isn't a critique – it's a coaching session. You're open to improvements and hungry for guidance. Trust creates a stage where honest conversations aren't threats; they're stepping stones to growth.

Ethical Compass in Action

Ethics and trust are like inseparable buddies. When trust flourishes, ethical decisions are on the menu. Everyone knows the same playbook, and the team follows it with gusto. Trust is the ingredient that turns each individual into an ethical superhero, safeguarding the organization's integrity.

Ditch the Micromanaging Habit

Imagine being given the trust keys to drive your work. No backseat driving, no constant supervision. Micromanaging, the trust killer, takes a hike. Trust blooms when you're given the reins to make decisions that drive success.

Hear the Voices of Your Team

Use surveys to tap into the collective wisdom of your team. Their ideas and suggestions become your biggest boon. Feedback flows both ways, creating a trust loop that nurtures growth.

The Fair Treatment Fertilizer

In the trust field, fairness is the sunlight that helps everything grow. When one person or team isn't treated fairly, trust wilts. Keep the trust garden lush by treating everyone equally, with explanations for decisions that might appear biased.

The Heartfelt Care Touch

Trust isn't just a workplace dance; it's a life waltz. Acknowledge that everyone has a life outside those office walls. Show genuine interest in their well-being. This nurturing attitude cultivates a space where honesty is the norm.

Lead by Trust Example

Trust-building starts at the top – that's you, leaders! Your actions set the tone. Be the beacon of trustworthiness, and your team members will follow suit. Trust cascades like a waterfall, shaping a culture where trust is currency.

Let the Truth Shine Bright

Remember, honesty is the spotlight, revealing everything, no matter how unflattering. Telling the whole truth, even when it's not all sunshine and rainbows, fuels the trust fire. Transparency trumps secrets any day.

Now, let's talk about the magic of high-trust organizations. These are places where innovation is the norm, where risk-taking isn't feared but embraced. High-trust organizations are like wonderlands where collaboration and communication flow freely.

And here's a mind-boggling stat: people in high-trust companies report a whopping 106% more energy at work.

Who knew trust could be the ultimate energy booster?

And leaders, you're at the crux of it all. Creating a safe space, being authentic, and delivering on promises are your trust-building instruments. The more trust you nurture, the more engaged, satisfied, and productive your team becomes. It's like a cycle of success that feeds on trust and flourishes in your leadership.

So, here's my call to action:

Before you hit the gas pedal on actions or let words fly out of your mouth, hit the brakes for a sec. Think it through, my friends.

Because let me be honest with you – sometimes the aftermath ain't what you wished for. Trust is like a rare gem; it's no easy catch, but boy, is it worth it. And the best part – it's absolutely free, but you gotta put in the elbow grease to earn it.

Chapter 5

Are You a Leader or a Follower?

"Sometimes you get to do what you want to do. The rest of the time, you do what you have to."

Leadership is a topic that really gets my gears turning!

Let's talk about leadership and how it's like donning the captain's hat in a vast sea of possibilities. I want you to understand the difference between being the guide and forging the path or simply following in someone else's footsteps.

The Leaders. The brainiacs, the wizards, the true movers and shakers of the world. The ones who have turned their brilliant ideas into household names like Google, Microsoft, Amazon, and Apple. We're talking about the folks who've sprinkled their magic into the products and messages that capture our attention.

Now, let's zoom in on a modern-day scenario. Take Instagram, for instance. You post something, and what's the first thing they ask you about?

Not how many leaders you have, but how many followers. It's like a world of followers out there!

But understand this: in a world that's spinning faster every day and new AI is marching in, the game is changing. We're all being nudged to step up and be leaders, even in our own lives.

It's about owning the steering wheel of your journey because, let's face it, some folks out there need a GPS to navigate their own lives.

For me, leadership is like that fabulous mixtape of mistakes and courage. It's about being able to raise your hand and say, "Hey, I got that wrong, but I'm not throwing in the towel just yet!"

When you're in the leadership spotlight, you're not trapped in a straightjacket. Nope, you can pivot, change your course, and learn from those oopsie moments.

Remember the wise words of Arnold Schwarzenegger?

"Keep moving forward, keep moving, moving."

It's like a marathon – you just keep chugging along, one step at a time.

So, my dear readers, whether you're leading the charge or happy to march to someone else's beat, remember this: the world is your playground. With each choice you make, each direction you take, every move you make, someone's watching you. Make it worth their while. Yes, there might be bumps and twists, but don't be afraid to veer off the beaten path.

Leadership, my friends, it's not about a fancy title or a corner office. It's about the interplay between your dreams and your actions. So, go out there and lead with your own style. Because when you're at the helm, the world is your oysters, waiting for your talent to be discovered.

Let's talk about a true legend, Winston Churchill. This guy was famous for a reason, and one of his gems of wisdom goes something like this:

"If you don't change your mind, you can't change anything."

And you know what? I wholeheartedly agree.

Now, we have to talk about changing your mind because it's not just about the change itself, but how you navigate through it, that really matters.

I've been passing down this golden nugget of insight to my kids since they were knee-high – you want to be a leader, not just a follower.

And here's why: imagine you're following someone, strolling along, and suddenly you realize you're on the road leading to nowhere good. It's like blindly walking into a never-ending pit. If you look south of the border, you might see this in full display.

Yep, I'm talking about a clear example of what happens when followers don't stop to think.

So, for goodness' sake, when you're young, aim to become your inner leader. It's like flexing your thinking muscles. Listen to others, absolutely, but don't drown in the cacophony of opinions out there.

A word of caution: be wary of that slippery slope known as "bullshit." Excuse my language, but it's the truth. It's like a toxic fog that clouds your judgment and can lead you astray.

Picture this: you're at a bustling amusement park, and you decide to join a group of friends headed to the roller coaster. You all hop in line, chatting, laughing, and generally having a great time.

Now, here's the twist. As you inch closer to the ride, you suddenly realize that your friends aren't waiting for the roller coaster; they're in line for the merry-go-round. It's all bright colors and gentle music, a far cry from the adrenaline-pumping loops and twists you were ready for.

You stand there, torn between sticking with your friends or following your own thrill-seeking instincts. That's the moment of truth, where you decide whether to be a follower or become your own leader of adventure.

So, listen up. Learn to dance to your own tune and think for yourself. Don't be bothered about what the world's saying; focus on what it's trying to tell you. Your heart knows the deal, trust me.

You see, changing direction isn't a mark of defeat. It's a sign of growth. And, oh boy, leaders make mistakes. They trip, stumble, and faceplant. It's part of the show. But the real magic is owning up to those blunders. That's the real act of leadership. It's like admitting you added salt to the pot instead of sugar. It's okay to mess up. Because that's the moment you level up, my friend.

You know, when I look at my kids, I'm not aiming for them to just be followers. I've got this strong belief that the younger generation is in no way useless. It's just that their minds have this different groove, a unique rhythm. They've got smarts that can light up a room, creativity that can paint the world in new shades, and education that fuels their aspirations. They're these fierce go-getters, and it's my duty to be their ultimate cheerleader. Not to dictate their lives, oh no, but to provide them with the trampoline they need to soar to their best lives, to make a commitment that echoes through time.

You know, when someone walks up to me with an idea that doesn't really resonate with me, my usual response is, "Now, that's an interesting thought." It's like a polite brush-off, a ninja move to dodge unnecessary debates.

My wife, well, she used to remind me that the "yes" stamp at work should probably make a guest appearance at home, too. She had a knack for leadership, no doubt. I remember this one time she asked me about Christmas wishes. I was all, "Honey, I don't really need anything. We've got plenty." But she wasn't having any of that. She quipped, "Come on, there's gotta be something you secretly want." I tried to slide her my credit card, but she was having none of that either. Now, that's leadership, plain and simple.

Being a leader doesn't mean I'm allergic to following other leaders. It's more about having this internal GPS that navigates me away from folks who are more followers than trailblazers. Trust me, you can spot those pure followers from a mile away, and you don't want to join that party. They're like this caravan with no clear destination, and you definitely don't want to end up going in circles.

There's a universe of wisdom packed into the world of leadership, and some of the best mentors come in the form of books, seminars, and people who've mastered the art. Way back when I signed up for the Dale Carnegie course, and yeah, I wasn't a fan. But looking back, I've got to tip my hat to it. Then there were these seminars with the remarkable Stephen Covey. Man, those were like brain workouts for leadership muscles. Oh, and my brother? He's a maestro at molding leaders. He had this knack for showing us the ropes and building bridges of leadership skills. He's still at it, a master of the trade. I even told him the other day, "Man, I should've hushed up and soaked in your wisdom more."

Everything we've been chatting about up to now is like building your leadership skills toolkit. Think of it as assembling your own superhero utility belt. But don't worry, there are no radioactive spider bites required. Just practice, my friend.

Give some of these ideas a whirl and watch the magic unfold.

Now, as a leader, you're bound to waltz into some clashes every now and then, just part of the gig. But don't fret. It's like a puzzle. Conflict is just a puzzle that's missing a few pieces. Step one: tune in, really listen. No need to get all caught up in a shouting match. I mean, seriously, that's like trying to untangle headphones in the dark – it's just not gonna end well. Start with a quick fix, sort out the immediate mess, and then think about the long game. And make sure to lean in and hear the other side. You've got your own thing, sure, but they've come into play, too.

So, ease up, lend an ear, and maybe, just maybe, you'll find some common ground.

Oh, and don't freak out if you realize you're not always the all-knowing oracle. It's cool. We're all just humans doing the best we can. Trust your gut, blend it with what you know, and don't let wild rumors twist your arm. Dig into the facts, and show them you're not just fiddling around. You really do care. Because if you don't, they'll probably just hit you with a "got it, moving on."

Remember, yes means yes. Well, this is a hard no.

Now you have to start over and make sure you understand the concern, break it down into chunks, and get agreement on small pieces. First, once you break it down, get a grip on small things, but don't give up when they go. Yeah, that means no.

This is where the real magic happens. These are the tools you need to solve those conflict conundrums. Dig deep, uncover the root cause, and wear your detective hat. And hey, don't let it linger. If consensus is playing hard to get, it's like being the captain of a ship. You've got to steer it yourself sometimes.

And remember, whether it's just you and your buddy or a whole squad, aim for consensus. But if the consensus doesn't work, and you've got to make a call, give them a heads-up – you're calling the shots. They might not throw you a parade, but hey, it's not a popularity contest. It's about pulling up those sleeves and working together, whether it's tackling a project or figuring out whose turn it is to take out the trash. Oh, and when it's family time, give a little more – love, time, and patience. Just remember, you're not out to win. You're here to team up, both in the world of business and in the coziness of your own home.

You know, the secret to creating leaders is pretty straightforward, actually. It's like handing them a treasure map with clear directions: "Here's what I expect. Here's what I'd like. Here's what I hope for." Then, the real magic? It's about stepping back, my friend, and letting them spread their wings. Think of it as giving them the stage, turning on the spotlight, and watching them own it. That's empowerment in action.

Of course, it's not a free-for-all carnival. We're talking disciplined support here. If you spot them veering off course, resist the urge to jump in and redirect their ship. No, no. Let them navigate their own waters. You've got bigger fish to fry, after all. So, don't micromanage, that's so last season. Give them the room to tinker, experiment, and maybe stumble a bit.

And no, this isn't just some fancy office strategy. This approach works in pretty much any scenario you can think of, whether it's cracking a tough nut at work or tackling a DIY project at home.

I've seen it a thousand times: people with good intentions handing someone a hammer and some pins, only to swoop in like a superhero at the slightest sign of a wobble. "Hold up, let me show you how it's done." But let me tell you, that's not the kind of leader we're aiming to be. That's like a magician showing you all the tricks before the grand reveal – it just takes away the magic.

Instead, be that wise sage who sits back and lets the show unfold. Imagine handing over the hammer, pointing to the holes and pins, and then quietly stepping aside. Let them pound away, even if it's a bit wonky at first. The trick is to let them figure it out, let them stumble upon the solutions.

You?

Well, you've got your own wizardry to attend to.

And you know what. This isn't some exclusive club where only the work matters. Nah, it's an all-access pass. Whether it's that tough case at the office or a disaster waiting to happen at home, the rules are the same. Let them flex their problem-solving skills. Let them be the architects of their own successes and, yes, their own fumbles. Because in the end, that's what true leadership is all about guiding from the shadows, nudging when needed, but ultimately letting them shine in their own spotlight.

So, whether you're chasing that degree or striding into the job market, leadership is your co-pilot. But hey, don't think it's confined to your professional avatar. Even beyond the nine-to-five, these skills are your trusty sidekick for those moments when you need to rally the troops and turn things around. Just imagine you're the hero of your own story, ready to conquer challenges and face difficulties with grace.

But leadership is not a one-size-fits-all label; it's a dynamic blend of who you are and the situations you face. You must have a unique leadership style. Yet, there are some qualities that every leader worth their salt shares – think of them as the ones that make a leader:

1. Accountability
2. Awareness
3. Confidence
4. Decisiveness
5. Empathy
6. Focus
7. Honesty
8. Inspiration
9. Optimism

So, why does leadership even matter?

Here are some reasons:

Initiating Action

Leaders are the ones who don't just draw the blueprints but roll up their sleeves and get the wheels turning. From outlining action plans to setting up the playfield, they're in the game.

Guiding Stars

If you're in a maze, and your leader is the compass. When things get tricky, they're there with a flashlight guiding your way. They're the unsung heroes who smooth out the bumps in your journey.

The Inspiration Genies

They are the poster models for motivation! Leaders aren't just about to-do lists. They're the ones who generate enthusiasm, turning ordinary tasks into extraordinary feats. A pat on the back, a glimpse of future growth – they make it happen.

The Confidence Charms

Ever felt like you're in a tricky spot? It's the leader to the rescue. They boost your morale when you hit rough patches. With their faith, you'll find courage even in uncharted waters.

Role Model Royalty

Leaders are the benchmark of behavior. Like a compass, they show the North Star of conduct. The best leaders know that humility and accountability are their trusty sidekicks.

The Consensus Collectors

As we talked earlier, they bring the team together. They bring all the opinions together, helping them toward progress. If decisions were a cake, they'd be the icing that binds the layers.

Talent Spotters

Leaders are the ones who spot the right pieces for the right spots. With their eagle eyes, they ensure that each talent shines where it's meant to.

The Public Faces

When the spotlight's on, leaders step up. They're not just managing tasks but presenting the organization in its best light.

Like a spokesperson, they're the ones who ensure the public sees the heart behind the hustle.

Now, you might wonder if leadership skills are genetically coded. Surprise, they're not! While some folks might have a knack for it, these skills are like seeds that can sprout into something incredible with the right care and attention. Yes, even if you're not born with a leadership gene, you can craft your own. All you need are the right tools and some good ol' nurturing.

So, how do you become a star leader?

Discipline Dynamo

Instill in yourself the willpower to meet deadlines or stick to commitments. It's a form of leadership discipline. Just keep at it and watch yourself grow.

Load Up on Responsibility

Ever felt like the weight of tasks fell squarely on your shoulders? Well, seek more of them. Taking on responsibilities, especially beyond your job description, is like training for the leadership marathon.

Ears Wide Open

Listening isn't just about hearing words; it's about absorbing the melody beneath them. As a leader, you'll need that. So, tune in, not just for the talk but for the meaning.

Big Picture Visionary

You must have deductive reasoning and the ability to anticipate twists. That's the leader's role, seeing the big picture, spotting possible bumps, and having ready-to-go solutions.

Motivation Maverick

Learn to applaud others and give them a standing ovation. If you appreciate words of encouragement, you must help others score touchdowns of success.

Lifelong Learner

Leadership isn't stagnant; it's like a river, always flowing. Be an avid learner. The more you know, the better you'll be at leading through the waves of change.

Delegate Dreamer

Sharing tasks isn't a sign of weakness; it's a symbol of strength. Leaders know when to pass the baton to the right team member and let them sprint with it.

Conflict Connoisseur

Conflict resolution – leaders are like the glue that fixes a broken vase. They know when to mend when to replace, and when to appreciate the mosaic of differences.

Diary of Progress

Ever kept a journal? Leaders do, too, not just for their musings but for their journey. Think of it like a treasure map where you mark X for accomplishments and O for opportunities.

Passion Detective

Leaders have the knack to find the X that marks the spot. When you're driven by what ignites your fire, leading becomes second nature.

Everyday Guru

Leadership isn't just a job; it's a way of life. Whether you're coordinating a school project or planning a weekend getaway, these skills melt into the core of your everyday choices.

Leaders are those guides who don't just wander but set our compasses to growth and authenticity. Whether it's raising kids or running companies, leadership is all about influence, empowerment, and making the world a bit brighter with our unique footprints. And remember, it's not about erasing followers but about empowering leaders, us included. So, let's rally, learn, and dare to orchestrate change, one decision at a time.

Chapter 6

Make Every Second Count

As we journey through life, from those early steps to the seasoned chapters, three constants are destined to shape our path. Drive. Knowledge. Experience

Here's the lowdown on what's guaranteed:

First, let's talk about the juice that keeps your engine revving – your Drive. Yep, that's your fire, your spark, your get-up-and-go. It's what gets you out of bed every dawn, ready to take on whatever the day throws your way.

Next up, knowledge. Think of it as the collection of puzzle pieces that gradually complete the big picture of life. It's like a treasure trove gathered from all around – school, parents, pals, mentors. With each nugget of wisdom, you're painting a richer portrait of the world.

And last but not least, the heavyweight champion – experience. This one's a marathon, not a sprint. It's the countless moments, the triumphs, the oopsies, and everything in between. As the years pile up, so does your treasure chest of experiences.

Now, let's dive into why this trio matters. Imagine your younger self, brimming with energy, curiosity, and a whole lot of "bring it on." You've got Drive in abundance, like a tank of high-octane fuel. But here's the catch – your knowledge bank is still a work in progress, and your experience shelf is only beginning to fill up.

As we keep truckin' on, life shifts its gears. Your Drive is still there, maybe a bit more polished, but no less potent. You're in the process of becoming a knowledge sponge, soaking up insights from all directions. It's like collecting gems from each encounter, storing them in your mental treasure chest.

Now, tie it all together. At this stage, you've got a toolbox equipped with Drive, knowledge, and a growing portfolio of experiences.

Remember, as you rock through life, you're not just a passive passenger; you're steering this ship. With your Drive as the engine, your knowledge as the compass, and your experiences as the sails catching the wind, you're charting your course.

"Learning this ain't gonna be cheap, but it's an investment."

Your mid to late 20s and early 30s is a time when experience starts piling up like laundry. You swear you'll fold, but don't. It's like a treasure hunt, and each year is a shiny new coin to add to your collection.

Here's the scoop, my friend: Life's handing you a limited-time offer: a buffet of Drive, a feast of knowledge, and a buffet of experiences, all served between the late 20s and early 50s.

I've been there, done that. In fact, my buddies and I hit our stride, hitting the gas pedal as if life were a grand race. We had this Drive, this relentless energy like the whole world was a racetrack, and we were in pole position. Those late-night brainstorms and endless cups of coffee?

Yeah, that was us pushing our limits and loving every minute of it.

A little wisdom from my father, when we joined him in the family business, he dropped the truth bomb: "Learning this ain't gonna be cheap, but it's an investment."

And let me tell you, it cost us – not just money but sweat, tears, and late nights burning the midnight oil. But leadership, the good kind, showed us the ropes, and we persevered. It wasn't a cakewalk, but our commitment matched our age, young and determined.

Fast-forward a few years. I'm now 65, wisdom lines etched on my face, a treasure trove of experience under my belt, and a bit too comfy in my armchair.

Here's the real talk, my friend – *lazy ain't the way to success.*

You can't just snooze your way to triumph. Trust me, I've tried. Success doesn't drop in your lap; you have to chase it down.

Now, let's shine a spotlight on these three legends and how to harness them: Drive, Knowledge, and Experience. They're like your trusty sidekicks, accompanying you on this wild journey called life.

Drive – that fiery passion that propels you out of bed, like your morning coffee with a turbo boost. It's that itch to conquer, to create, to make your mark on the world. Keep that fire alive; it's like rocket fuel for your dreams.

Knowledge –the ultimate power-up. Think of it as your secret weapon, a sword in your scabbard. It's not just book smarts. It's the bits of wisdom you gather from the world, your mentors, your stumbles, and your triumphs. It's your treasure map to navigate the maze.

Experience –the grand storyteller. Every scar, every laugh, every "Oops, did I really do that?" adds a chapter to your life's novel. It's like your true north, guiding you away from pitfalls and towards possibilities.

So here's the deal, my friend. Life's handing you the keys to a dazzling ride, and those keys have three magical trinkets: Drive, Knowledge, and Experience. They're yours to wield, to steer, to turn into your epic tale.

The Power of Three

I've always had a soft spot for those folks who don't play the delay game. The fight off the Godzilla of procrastination. You know, the type they tackle whatever's in front of them head-on, no dilly-dallying. As for me, I've had my fair share of wrestling with the art of not putting things off.

Procrastination is actually a fancy term for "I'll do it later."

Let's face it: it's a sneaky monster that can creep into our lives without us even realizing it. Unless you're part of the elite "Get Things Done Right Now" club, like a superhero of productivity, you've got to fight to keep that procrastination monster at bay.

So, here's my approach: the power of three. I find that taking on three problems or tasks at a time is a solid strategy. Anything more, and it's like piling up a towering sandwich with too many layers, it just becomes a chaotic mess.

See, the tricky thing about procrastination is that it often preys on the things that don't seem hard but are oh-so-necessary. We've all been there, right? Starting something and then, well, life happens. This is where things get messy. I've seen it countless times: people start something, and then boom, it's like they got caught in a time warp.

Here's the thing: Most people you ask will tell you they're busier than a bee at a flower farm. And it's often because they've left a trail of unfinished business behind. Trust me, that half-done to-do list is like a jackhammer in your head, noisy and downright irritating.

I've been in that boat, my friend. I'd create this folder of things I needed to tackle right now, and I'd feel like a champ when I kept it empty. But, oh boy, the times when I let it pile up? Stress implosion.

Remember that old saying?

"Three steps forward, two steps back." It's like a dance of progress. It's part of the whole gig of growing, of learning, of gathering Knowledge and Experience like precious gems.

Leadership – Oh yeah, it's in the mix too. See, a leader doesn't just lead others; they've got to lead themselves. That means picking up the bouncing ball when it slips off the table and putting it back on track. Simple as that.

Now, imagine this scenario: you're in that procrastination maze, and suddenly, you realize – "Hey, I've caught up! Wait, that was quick. I just burnt a bunch of energy for nothing." See, that's the thing about procrastination – it's like a sneaky energy thief. If you're not careful, it can mess with your Drive, that fuel that keeps your engine running.

We all find ourselves in its clutches, caught between what we should do and what we'd rather not. But fear not, for in this whirlwind of shoulds and should-nots, there lies a path to break free, to dance to your own tune of accomplishment.

That nagging list of tasks you've been avoiding, asking for that overdue raise, approaching that enchanting someone, or even just making that overdue call to Mom. You see, the thing is, our brains tend to lean towards pleasure and comfort, sidestepping the harder, less enjoyable tasks. It's like choosing a cozy couch over a treadmill; we're wired to seek immediate gratification.

But guess what?

Beneath this deceptively appealing facade lies the harsh truth: avoiding those tasks often ends up causing more misery than facing them head-on.

So, how do we break the spell? How do we stop procrastinating and finally tip the scales in favor of productivity?

Let's start with the simplest of moves – the "Tiny Step Shuffle."

Imagine you need to write a report that's been looming over you like a storm cloud. Rather than being overwhelmed by the thunder and lightning, start with a single word. Literally, just one word. It's like sticking your toe in the water before diving in. Once you dip your toe, that storm might not seem so daunting anymore.

How about creating an environment that makes it harder to procrastinate than to actually do the task? Think about it – if you want to work out, invest in a gym membership or schedule those classes. Suddenly, the fear of losing money becomes a bigger motivator than the dread of exercise.

Ever heard of the *"Do Something Principle"*?

It's like the gateway drug to productivity. Tell yourself, "Just open a blank document and write the first sentence." Before you know it, you'll find yourself breezing through the next few lines. It's like a snowball effect; action breeds motivation, and motivation fuels more action.

Now, let's talk about that psychological boogeyman – fear. You see, behind our most stubborn procrastination often lurks a fear. It might be a fear of failure, of success, of change, or even of hurting someone else. These fears wrap themselves around our identity like vines, making it feel like we're trading our sense of self for progress.

Imagine a friend trapped in this cycle of avoidance, dreaming of sharing their art online but never quite hitting that launch button. The fear of being an artist, of revealing their true self, holds them hostage. Sound familiar? It's a tale as old as time, the battle between who we are and who we wish to become.

Now, here's a twist: let go of these tight grips on grandiosity. Embrace the ordinary and redefine yourself in simpler terms. See yourself not as a superstar or a failure but as a student, a partner, a friend, or a creator. You see, the more grandiose our self-identity, the more the prospect of change threatens it. Strip away the layers, and suddenly, the fears melt like snow in spring.

Let me be clear: this isn't a one-step dance. It's a routine, a commitment to taking those small steps even when the fear tugs at you. Remember, perfect action is not the goal – it's progress. In the grand theater of life, imperfect action beats the hollow applause of inaction any day.

Make Every Second Count

In life, one thing that often takes center stage is time. Now, time's a tricky fellow, isn't it? Not just yours, mind you, but the time of those around you. And this, my friends, is where the secret sauce of good leadership begins: punctuality.

Now, great leaders, those folks you admire, the ones who radiate "I've got this" vibes – they're the masters of being on time. Trust me, it's not just about catching the right train; it's about catching the essence of respect.

Here's the deal: grasp this early in the game, and it's like having a golden key that unlocks a treasure chest of respect and credibility. Being late, well, that's like sending out an "I don't care about your time" message. And let's be real – that's not the impression we want to leave, right?

Now, the tricky part is once you've earned the "latecomer" label, shaking it off is like trying to peel off a stubborn sticker, not easy, my friend. And let's face it, dealing with that label just adds to the list of things life throws at us.

So why not steer clear of this messy maze?

Being on time doesn't mean you have to sprint to every appointment. Give yourself a little cushion, a buffer for those curveballs' life likes to throw. That way, you're not just punctual; you're that composed and collected individual who's got their game face on.

Now, let's chat about baggage. And no, I'm not talking about lugging around suitcases. I mean the non-tangible stuff, the things that weigh you down. We've all been there, haven't we? People who drag us into the drama abyss or those negative vibes that linger like unwelcome guests.

It's the art of reviewing, taking a moment to peek into your day, your week, your month, heck, even your year. In your head, imagine two lists. On one side, you jot down the good vibes, the accomplishments, the things that make you go, "Heck yeah!" On the other, you scribble down the stuff that's been a bit of a downer.

Guess what? You've got a choice.

Hold on to the positives like precious gems, and then, here's the superhero move – face the negatives head-on. It's like decluttering your mental space, making room for the good stuff.

It's simple, really. Be on time, not just for your appointments but for respect. Toss the baggage that's like a lead weight around your progress. And hey, take a moment to reflect, to sift through the day's happenings and shape your focus.

How to Boost Productivity

The ever-elusive quest for a day of uninterrupted productivity is a tale as old as the snooze button. We all know the struggle. You wake up determined to conquer your to-do list, but before you can even say "caffeine," distractions come barging in like party crashers at a library. You try to juggle flaming torches while riding a unicycle on a tightrope – entertaining but hardly productive.

I'm here to guide you through the treacherous landscape of modern productivity pitfalls. In a world where notifications are as common as the air we breathe, it's time to put on your focus armor and charge into the fray.

The Siren Song of Interruptions

So you're sitting at your desk, ready to conquer the world, or at least that looming report. But wait, your phone buzzes. It's a notification. It could be important, right?

Maybe it's your friend's cat doing something "adorable" again. So, you give in and take a peek. An hour later, you've seen three videos about cats wearing tiny hats, watched a TED talk about the art of folding socks, and somehow ended up reading conspiracy theories about time-traveling hamsters. Sound familiar?

We've all fallen into the notification trap. Our smartphones ping and buzz, and suddenly, we're wandering down distraction alley, far from the productive path. But remember, you're the navigator of your own ship – set those notifications to "Do Not Disturb" and steer your focus back on course.

The Battle Plan: 10 Tips for Distraction Defiance

1. Have a Battle Plan the Night Before

Before the sun sets on your day, chart your course for the next. Write down two essential tasks that must be slain to claim victory. And remember, even if the first task turns out to be a tricky dragon, the second will be there to back you up. Start your day with these quests, and only then consider the siren call of emails and social media.

2. Conquer the Distractions

Why let distractions pillage your focus? Take control! Silence your notifications, tame your smartphone, and keep emails at bay. Instead of being at the beck and call of your devices, become their master. Check your inbox only at designated times, and soon, you'll be the captain of your attention, steering through the calm waters of productivity.

3. Find Your Focus Comfort Zone

Productivity isn't one-size-fits-all; it's a custom-made armor that suits only you. Whether it's a particular chair, soothing music, or a perfectly brewed cup of tea, create an environment where you can channel your inner task-slaying champion. Find what makes you comfortable and focused, like a knight donning their trusted armor before heading into battle.

4. Embrace the Zen of Meditation

Imagine you sitting in serene silence, your mind as calm as a mountain lake. Meditation isn't just for yogis. It's your secret weapon against the invading army of interruptions. Even just a few minutes a day can help you vanquish those wandering thoughts and return to your focus fortress.

5. Divide and Conquer Your Goals

Big goals are like mountains, awe-inspiring, but climbing them can feel overwhelming. Chop those peaks into smaller foothills. Each conquered foothill brings you closer to the summit of productivity. A focused sprint uphill, rather than a distracted marathon on the plains, is the key to reaching the peak.

6. Sweet Slumber, the Elixir of Focus

Sleep is the magical elixir that rejuvenates your focus and ignites your creativity. Don't let the illusion of productivity tempt you into sacrificing precious sleep hours. Remember, a well-rested warrior wields their sword of focus with unmatched skill.

7. Visual Battle Cries

Harness the power of visual reminders. Stick a note on your monitor that screams "Focus, Focus, Focus!" Let it be your battle cry against the distractions lurking in the shadows. When the allure of social media beckons, a quick glance at your reminder will set you back on track.

8. Celebrate Small Victories

Who doesn't love a reward? Finish a task, and claim your prize. Whether it's a quick snack, a stroll in the park, or a sneak peek at your social media feed, these rewards will be your motivation to stay on task and accomplish your goals.

9. March to the Rhythm of Breaks

Even the mightiest warrior needs a breather. Stand up, stretch those limbs, and step away from your battlefield. A short walk or a few minutes of fresh air can recharge your focus and prepare you for your next conquest.

10. Unplug and Unleash

Free your mind by detaching from work for a while. Engage in non-screen activities, work out, go for a run, play a sport, solve puzzles, or indulge in a game of chess. Remember, a healthy body is the stronghold of a focused mind.

Navigating Distractions like a Pro

So your alarm clock chimes, and you rise with a sense of purpose. You're not just tackling tasks; you're conquering them. The pings and buzzes of the digital realm don't faze you. You've tamed the distraction dragon. Your focus is sharper than a sword's edge, and your productivity is a force to be reckoned with.

Time Is of the Essence

Let's explore the art of time management. Trust me, it's not just about scheduling like a robot. It's about crafting a solution of efficiency, less stress, and more "heck yeah, I nailed it" moments.

Know Your Hours

Imagine your time as a precious resource, like those gold coins in a video game. You wouldn't want to spend them on things that don't level you up, right? So, arm yourself with a time-tracking tool. *RescueTime's* your trusty sidekick here. It'll show where your hours are: dancing, work, or the non-stop social media fiesta. Analyze, adapt, and kick those distractions to the curb.

Stick to a Schedule

Daily schedules do not need to be boring and rigid but a flexible roadmap to success. Create time blocks for tasks. You're basically planning your day. Make sure to keep it real. Ever heard of the "planning fallacy"? We're all victims. Leave room for unexpected dragons and monster emails that need slaying.

Prioritize Like a Pro

You've got a mountain of tasks. Big ones, small ones, and those ninja ones that keep pouncing out of nowhere. Enter the Eisenhower Matrix, your mystical guide. It's all about importance and urgency. Defeat the tasks that are crucial and have a ticking clock first. Delegate the minions, delay the wizards, and vanquish the irrelevant.

Tackle the Monstrous Task

Again, the beast of procrastination – we all know it too well. But what if I told you there's a potion to banish it? It's called "Eat That Frog." The idea is simple: face the biggest, ugliest, slimiest task first thing in the morning. You see when you've gulped down the frog, the rest of your day is a breeze of triumphs.

Batch It Up

Grouping similar tasks is like combining ingredients for a magical potion. Batch process like a pro. Have client meetings on specific days, respond to emails at designated hours, and generate reports all at once. You'll ride the wave of efficiency, my friend.

The Time Illusionist

Have you ever noticed how tasks swell to fill the time you give them? Enter Parkinson's Law, the time wizard. Trick it! Give tasks a time cap. If you thought a report would take all day, watch how it moves faster when you tell it, "You've got two hours, pal."

Boundaries: Learn to Say No

Your energy is like the coin pouch of a brave adventurer – finite. So, wield the magic of "no." Guard your focus like a dragon guards its treasure. Focus on your strengths, delegate to allies, and protect your castle of productivity.

Avoid Multitasking

Juggling tasks is no joke. Your brain isn't a circus act. Science says multitasking is a myth that chops productivity like a woodcutter on a mission. Focus on one task at a time. It's like a laser beam of productivity.

Keep Your Space Organized

A cluttered battlefield is a recipe for chaos. Organize like you're leveling up in a game. Clear your desk of the documents that don't spark joy. Organize your files so you don't spend ages searching. And keep your calendar crystal clear.

Wield Productivity Tools

Harness the power of digital relics – productivity tools. *Slack* for team telepathy, *Dropbox* for the virtual treasure chest of files, and *Google/Outlook Calendar* for time travel. These tools work like magic to boost your efficiency.

I want you to embrace punctuality like an old friend, kick that baggage to the curb, and keep your positivity game strong. After all, life's a wild ride, and showing up on time is like securing the best seat in the house. Time waits for no one, but when you're on its wavelength, it sure does give you a nod of approval.

So, dear reader, let's step onto the floor and face procrastination with grace. Start small, create an environment that nudges you toward action, and redefine your self-identity with humility. Let's trade the temporary allure of comfort for the lasting satisfaction of accomplishment. The curtain's up, the music's playing and the spotlight's on you. It's time to master the art of stopping procrastination and write your story of triumph.

Also, remember, age isn't just a number. It's a chapter, a phase, a seasoning that adds flavor to your journey. So ride that wave, harness that energy, learn like there's no tomorrow, and let experience be your guide.

And when you find yourself contemplating a cozy spot in that armchair, remind yourself – you've got a trio of wonders on your side. Being lazy is not an option. Keep the fire alive, keep the wisdom flowing, and keep living that story worth telling.

Chapter 7

Learning As We Go

Now, we have to talk about learning.

It's like a magic potion that transforms you into a better version of yourself. Learning is a process, my friends, one that leads to change, fueled by experience, and sets the stage for improved performance and future enlightenment.

A good education is like having a turbocharger for your brain. It's the express route to understanding and mastering new concepts. You absorb knowledge faster, like a sponge soaking up a spilled potion. So, if you ever wondered why your older brother and your youngest sibling, both armed with university degrees, are soaring in their endeavors, well, it's not a coincidence.

Now, let's talk about my journey. My brother David and I took a different route. We reached the respectable shores of Grade 12 and gained a different kind of wisdom - StreetSmarts.

It served us well, but here's the sage advice I have for you: *get yourself a solid education*. It's an investment that keeps on giving, like your personal bag of wisdom that you can dig into for years to come.

Here's a little story to give you some perspective. Once, my two brothers and I were in business with our father, and things were looking rosy. We were raking in the gold, basking in our success. We each had a decade's worth of experience under our belts, and we thought we were invincible. But you know what Dad said?

He took us to the window. We lived in Calgary, which has mountains like Denver, so he pointed at the mountains in the distance and dropped some knowledge bombs.

"Not one of those mountains goes up forever," he said, his eyes as serious as a scholar in a library. *"They all have a peak, and then they slope down."*

We exchanged glances, and it hit us like a lightning bolt. He was reminding us to be prepared for the downturns in life, both in business and beyond.

Life, he said, is a lot like those mountains — full of ups and downs. So, we nodded in agreement and got back to work, wiser and more determined than ever.

You see, folks, throughout your lifetime, you'll get nudged by reminders. Reminders that in your business endeavors, you'll encounter peaks and valleys, but it's how you manage the downs that truly matters.

And in your personal life, well, you'll quickly realize you don't have all the answers. That's when learning becomes your trusty sidekick. It's a continuous process, my friends, and there's always more to discover.

I want to share a story with you, a curveball I never anticipated having to navigate. It's a story that took me by surprise, challenging my assumptions about what I thought I knew.

It was December 2011, and my family and I were living in Victoria, British Columbia. We'd only been there for about a year, settling into our beautiful new home on the serene West Coast of Canada. Life was unfolding as we had imagined.

One morning, as Charlene, my wife, was getting ready, I found myself in my office just outside our bedroom. Suddenly, she called out, "Honey, come in here." My heart raced, and I couldn't help but think I was in some sort of trouble.

As I entered the room, I saw Charlene applying lotion, her face riddled with concern. Her hand rested on the top of her right breast, where she had discovered a small, hard lump. It was about the size of your smallest fingernail. At that moment, we both gasped in disbelief.

We were faced with a challenging question: *Now what?*

Fear and uncertainty flooded our thoughts. My immediate response was to call the doctor as soon as possible. And that's precisely what we did. We managed to secure an appointment that very day.

Our doctor, though not overly alarmed, ordered an ultrasound and some blood work. It was a whirlwind of medical appointments and anxious waiting. This is how swiftly life can change its course. Charlene was only 47 years old at the time, and I was 52. We couldn't fathom how something like this could happen to us, to her.

But it was happening, and we were thrust into a world we knew nothing about: breast cancer. We were hit with the hard truth, learning that this disease doesn't discriminate based on age or health. Charlene was young, vibrant, and in good health, with a precious 3.5-year-old daughter named Caitlyn. Our nanny, Andrea, who had joined our family just a few months prior, remained steadfast with Caitlyn throughout this challenging period, and she is still with her now.

I'm busier than I've ever been, dealing with stress levels that surpass anything I experienced during my 30-plus years in the trucking business.

The turning point came when Charlene received a diagnosis that shook our world to its core. It was triple-negative breast cancer, considered one of the most aggressive forms. We started this arduous journey in January 2011 with a six-month course of chemotherapy. The hope was to shrink the tumor before surgery, a tumor that was growing at an alarming pace. Looking back, I sometimes wonder if we should have pushed for surgery first, but hindsight offers no solace.

The chemo didn't yield the results we desperately needed. And so, Charlene underwent a double mastectomy, a surgery that marked a pivotal moment in our battle. But the challenges persisted. Radiation treatment left her with painful burns that seared through her back. At every clinic visit, we seemed to face grim news. In our quest for hope and healing, we explored alternative medicines, even venturing to Switzerland, where they bravely attempted to rebuild her immune system.

After nearly a month abroad, we returned home in October 2011, hopeful for a change in our fortunes. However, our return was met with devastating news. A CT scan at the cancer clinic revealed the cruel truth—cancer had metastasized, spreading to her back and lungs. The battle had taken an even darker turn.

In our darkest moments, we sought peace and spiritual guidance. We turned to our faith, to the church, and asked if we could have Caitlyn baptized, our precious 4-and-a-half-year-old daughter. Time felt incredibly scarce, and we needed to ensure that Caitlyn knew her mother's love, even in her absence. The minister at our local church, understanding the urgency, agreed.

I'll never forget the day. I took Caitlyn into our bedroom, and we sat in those comfortable chairs overlooking the tranquil ocean. I held her close and gently explained, *"Mommy isn't sick anymore. She's gone to see Grandma Mary in heaven."* The mixture of joy at the thought of her mom's relief from pain and the crushing realization of her absence was a weight too heavy for such a young heart.

In that moment, I learned that even the toughest among us can have a breaking point. My own heart ached with a pain I had never known before. The toughest task I ever faced was telling Caitlyn about her mother's passing, and it's a memory that will forever stay with me.

Life, as we discovered, can be achingly cruel at times. It tests us in ways we could never anticipate. But from this painful chapter, I learned one vital lesson: *in life's most trying moments, we unearth the most profound teachings.*

So, remember, my friends, that our lessons aren't always wrapped in joy; sometimes, they come shrouded in hardship. Cherish the knowledge you gain during the good times, and hold it close, for it will be your guide through life's unexpected twists and turns.

The takeaway from this unexpected twist in our lives is that learning can come from the most unexpected sources. It's in those moments of uncertainty, fear, and challenge that we discover our true strength. We learned about breast cancer, yes, but we also learned about adapting to circumstances, the power of support, and the importance of cherishing each day.

Grief is a profound aspect of the human experience, one that isn't always categorized as a mental health issue but leaves an indelible mark on our psyche. It's a subject we need to explore more deeply. I often wonder why grief education isn't an integral part of our national curriculum; it should be.

Losing your life partner is an experience that you can't escape, whether in the mind or the practicalities of daily existence. Humans are inherently wired to be part of a pair, and suddenly, finding yourself single is a transformation that's challenging to express in words. I remember feeling existentially alone for many years despite the presence of a loving family and supportive friends.

For those fortunate enough to access therapy, it becomes a space to share these complex emotions. Grief operates on its own agonizing timeline, one that you have to live through to truly comprehend. The death of the person you shared your life with is especially devastating because their presence lingers everywhere. Their DNA on the cups you sip from, the scent of their clothes in the closet — these sensations remain invisible to the outside world.

Yet, a bereaved individual isn't just one person; someone loved you deeply, and you continue to love them. After their passing, my love for Charlene remained as deep as it had been in life. Her physical presence was gone, but our bond, our commitment, remained unbroken.

However, the right to continue existing as part of a couple is often misunderstood by those who haven't walked this path of loss. In reality, the sensation of being in a couple can endure for years, decades, or even a lifetime. I view this connection as sacred and believe it should be respected. Yet, for other couples, bereaved spouses can be challenging to engage with. Their sadness, their sense of being *"half a couple,"* can feel burdensome.

Are they a threat, a reminder of life's fragility?

Meanwhile, the grieving partner needs to learn that the new life they build can coexist with the sorrow of what's lost. The experience of losing a life partner leaves behind a vast, bottomless pit filled with dark shadows that catch us by surprise like sharp, painful objects, causing us to stumble and wound ourselves. These objects are memories, and they reappear unexpectedly after a loved one has passed, different from memories of someone still living.

Letting go takes on a unique texture, distinct from the ties we sever because love has waned. When someone dies and their love for you remains, there's a survivor's guilt, a realization that you have a life while they remain immobilized.

Above all, we must honor the union that once was, acknowledging that they were one of two.

In the most ordinary and unassuming ways, memories haunt differently when you're alone. Shared memories have a different resonance. A widower's recollection of a wedding anniversary, for instance, can be challenging to celebrate with others without it feeling contrived.

What can you remember? Her birthday? The first time you laid eyes on her? Their first meal, holiday, engagement? It's a complex process when experienced in solitude. Whom do these private reflections and recollections serve? Without sharing, they can inflict pain.

Grief experts often encourage us to find strength, power, *"silver linings,"* and courage in our experiences. Most of us choose to continue, even in the bleakest moments, because the death instinct remains elusive in life. We wait for change, for a flicker of light in the darkness.

I believe that that flicker of light is learning. I believe that people have to learn new things and be open to new experiences in order to move on from the grief and survive, well not just survive, but eventually thrive in life.

Learning Is A Band-aid For Grief

There is something you must remember. Historically, humans have evolved through collective learning, passing knowledge down the generations. Our ancestors communicated and shared wisdom, parents taught children through observation, and students learned from their teachers' demonstrations. Interestingly, many students find complex subjects easier to grasp when explained by their peers, who often break things down more simply, a concept famously endorsed by Albert Einstein.

When one imparts knowledge to another, they're essentially passing on their wisdom verbally. The recipient might further share or integrate this knowledge into their projects—a fascinating cycle.

Remember, people around you are a source of wisdom, even if they aren't acclaimed authors or scholars. Learning can come from unexpected places.

Now, here's a fundamental truth: you'll never exhaustively grasp everything about anything. Pursuing knowledge is similar to diving into a rabbit hole, with each question birthing several more. The goal isn't to master a subject entirely but to focus on the information that serves your immediate purpose. You'll have a lifetime to delve deeper into your areas of interest.

We're perpetual students, forever exploring and forming connections with subjects. There's no end to the web of knowledge we can weave within a single subject, let alone across all subjects. This concept might provoke existential musings, but it's essential to acknowledge.

Learning, however, includes repetition. Just like practicing a new skill, revisiting knowledge solidifies it in your memory. As with your smartphone's limited storage space, your brain has limits too. You need to revisit concepts to reinforce them. Repetition is the key to effective learning.

Your brain is a dynamic organ that continues to learn throughout your life. *Neuroplasticity* is the term for this remarkable adaptability. Challenging your brain with new information enhances its capacity to acquire and process knowledge. In essence, you get smarter by actively learning.

This neural evolution occurs because new information strengthens your synapses, the connections between neurons. When you learn something new, you create fresh synapses, rewiring your brain to adapt to new circumstances. This happens daily and can be further encouraged and stimulated.

So, how can you nourish your brain's hunger for learning?

Travel, explore diverse cultures, learn a new musical instrument or language, read voraciously (especially materials that challenge you), and jot down notes. Revisit these notes whenever necessary, reinforcing your mental capacity.

Learning also thrives on the synergy of ideas, like borrowing insights from various sources and merging them into your understanding.

Life Skills Are Like Superpowers

Learning essential life skills helps you move forward and teaches you to be battle-ready when push comes to shove.

Life skills are like your personal superpowers; they're the essential abilities that help you conquer everyday tasks and navigate life's twists and turns. These skills aren't just about getting by – they're about thriving in both your personal and professional life. When you master them, you boost your self-confidence, increase your self-reliance, and gain a greater sense of control as you chase your dreams.

Think of them as your toolkit for life. These skills range from critical thinking and problem-solving to self-awareness and self-compassion. They're the Swiss Army knife of personal development, and they're crucial for your journey through life.

So, why are life skills so important?

Well, if life is like a grand adventure full of surprises, challenges, and opportunities, then having strong life skills is like having a trusty compass and a versatile map for this adventure. It helps you adapt, overcome obstacles, and confidently steer your course.

Experts usually group life skills into three broad categories: communication, coping, and decision-making. These categories encompass the essential tools we all need to make wise choices, handle daily challenges, and function effectively in society.

Let's break them down:

Communication Skills

These are the foundations of successful interactions. Being able to express yourself clearly and understand what others are saying is at the heart of effective communication. It's like a secret language that opens doors to collaboration, enriches relationships, and helps you set boundaries. Communication skills include verbal and written communication, emotional expression, active listening, and even nonverbal cues.

Coping Skills

Life can throw curveballs at you, and coping skills are your way of gracefully catching and throwing them back. These skills are all about recognizing and managing your emotions, which sets you on the path to controlling your life. With strong coping mechanisms, you can bounce back from setbacks, set meaningful goals, and develop a sense of security. They include self-esteem, self-awareness, and self-discipline.

Decision-Making Skills

Life is a series of choices, from career moves to family decisions. Your decision-making skills are like your true north, guiding you toward the right path. These skills involve problem-solving, critical thinking, and knowing when to seek help from trusted friends or mentors.

Critical Thinking

Critical thinking is like a mental gym workout. It's about examining things critically, from news articles to your own actions. It helps you read between the lines, evaluate complex issues, and make informed decisions. Whether you're leading a team or facing personal dilemmas, critical thinking helps you find creative solutions.

Technology Skills

In our digital age, tech skills are a must. It's not just about sending emails; it's about navigating the digital landscape, from managing online calendars to securing your digital life. These skills keep you organized and efficient.

Confidence

Confidence is your superpower. It's not about being arrogant; it's about recognizing your own worth and accepting feedback gracefully. Confidence empowers you to pursue opportunities, even when you're outside your comfort zone.

Empathy

Understanding others' perspectives is like wearing empathy glasses. It helps you build strong relationships, resolve conflicts, and lead teams effectively. Empathy brings trust and positivity, even in challenging situations.

Creativity

Creativity is your innovation engine. It's the key to finding unique solutions and approaching problems from new angles. Whether at work or in your personal life, creativity makes you a problem-solving maestro.

Adaptability

Change is the only constant in life, and adaptability is your super suit for dealing with it. Being open to new ideas and situations helps you navigate unexpected twists with grace.

Now, here's the fun part: improving your life skills. It's like leveling up in a video game; there's always room for growth. Here are some tips I have for you:

1. Be Curious: Channel your inner Sherlock Holmes. Ask questions, seek answers, and stay open to learning new things.

2. Find Mentors: Learn from the best. Seek guidance from people who inspire you. They'll help you grow both personally and professionally.

3. Look Inward: Self-reflection is your secret weapon. Take time to evaluate yourself, your emotions, and areas in your life that need attention.

4. Seek Learning Opportunities: Growth doesn't come knocking; you must go out and find it. Pursue your interests, take classes, and connect with like-minded individuals.

Lastly, be open to the discomfort of unfamiliarity. Challenge your biases and step outside your comfort zone. Don't dismiss what you haven't experienced; curiosity can lead to amazing learning experiences.

Equate life with purpose, seeking knowledge in every conversation, connection, and experience. Watch movies, take notes, write, read, listen, and travel. Feel deeply, ask questions, and find deeper meanings in everything you encounter.

Above all, leave a legacy. You never know how many people could become smarter because of you!

Chapter 8

Never Give Up!

Money Makes You More Comfortable.

Let's dive into a candid conversation about money. It's a topic that often dances in the shadows, but it's high time we shed some light on it.

First and foremost, let's talk about the absolute essentials: food, water, and shelter. These are the building blocks of life, the ABCs of survival.

Imagine you're out for dinner, and suddenly it hits you — why not pack your lunch instead? Or how about those outings? Why not choose the places that don't dent your wallet?

So, here's the deal: I encourage you to take a moment and calculate precisely how much these basics cost in your life. This is your starting point, your financial bedrock. It's where your transformation begins.

Now, let's bust a common myth: money doesn't buy happiness. It won't magically make you healthier, either. But what it can do is provide comfort. It's like a cozy blanket on a chilly evening; it won't solve all your problems, but it can make life a bit more comfortable.

Think of money as a tool, not the end goal. It's a means to an end, a facilitator of experiences and opportunities. It's what allows you to enjoy that dinner out or take that exciting trip without constantly worrying about your bank balance. It won't make your problems disappear with a flick of a wand, but it sure as heck would make them less intimidating.

They studied the choices made by over 1,000 graduating students from the University of British Columbia. They wanted to know whether they leaned toward valuing time or money as they set out into the world. The results were intriguing: most of these young minds leaned slightly towards cherishing time, but not by a significant margin. Nearly 40% of them were inclined to prioritize money.

So, how did this choice shape their mental and emotional well-being?

They measured their happiness levels both before graduation and one year after. To gauge their life satisfaction, they asked a simple question: "Taking all things together, how happy would you say you are?" They responded on a scale from 0 (not at all) to 10 (extremely).

The findings were striking. Those students who gave more weight to money ended up less happy a year after graduation compared to their peers who favored time. Even when they accounted for their happiness levels before graduation and considered their various socioeconomic backgrounds, the results remained consistent.

Now, don't get me wrong; this doesn't mean you should turn down a well-deserved raise. I've got plenty of evidence indicating that, on average, wealthier individuals tend to be happier. However, it's important to note that amassing wealth doesn't guarantee happiness. It's not just about making money; it's about how you handle it, how you save, and how you think about money that influences the joy it brings.

Now, I understand that saving money can be downright scary. Thoughts of cutting back, crafting meticulous budgets, and making sacrifices might give you a headache.

So, let's take a different approach, shall we? Start by asking yourself two fundamental questions:

1. What am I spending money on that isn't essential for my survival?

2. Does this expense genuinely contribute to my happiness?

If the answer to the second question is *"no,"* consider taking a break from those expenses, even if it's just for a few weeks. However, if an expense truly brings you joy, don't hesitate to enjoy it without any guilt. Let me show you some ways you can make mindful spending choices that are most likely to boost your happiness.

The Right Way to Spend Money (For a Happier You)

Invest in Experiences, Not Things

It's easy to fall into the trap of buying material things because they're easily comparable. The ease of comparison is precisely why material things often fall short of delivering lasting satisfaction. Experiences, on the other hand, are less comparable and tend to leave a more lasting imprint on our happiness.

Buy Yourself Some Time

In our fast-paced lives, finding time for enjoyable experiences can be a challenge, especially when we're juggling numerous responsibilities. However, the gig economy has made it more accessible and affordable for many to purchase a bit of free time.

Remarkably, spending money to buy yourself time actually elevates happiness levels. In a study conducted in 2017, participants received $40 to spend on either a time-saving purchase or a material item on two different weekends. Those who opted for time-saving experienced improved moods and reduced feelings of time pressure compared to those who went for material goods. Yet, when asked how they would spend a $40 windfall, only 2% planned to make a time-saving purchase.

Invest in Others

Try this little experiment: take a $10 or $20 bill and use it to benefit someone else today. You could send a small gift to a friend, help a stranger short on cash at the grocery store, or make a donation to a charity close to your heart. While it might be tempting to spend that money on yourself, a decade's worth of research suggests you're more likely to find happiness in spending it on others. This holds true even for those struggling to meet their own basic needs; the act of giving generates a "warm glow" in many.

However, the happiness derived from giving hinges on how and why you give. It's necessary that you view your decision to give as a choice rather than feeling pressured by someone to do it. Look for opportunities to give where you can see the impact of your generosity on a person or cause that genuinely matters to you. It's perfectly fine to start small; believe me, even a few dollars can lift your spirits.

Remember, happiness isn't about passively consuming pleasures. You need to discover activities that immerse you in the moment. But I'm not talking about vices.

You know, we've all come across some seriously wealthy folks in our lives. They've got it all, or so it seems. But here's what lies behind the facade: when they're gone, they don't take any of it with them. Money can't be your travel companion to the great beyond.

That's precisely why I've spent a considerable chunk of my time talking about prevention – just simple steps that light up the path to a healthier life. Now, let's get one thing straight: smoking, drinking, and drugs?

Chuck them. They don't belong in the prevention toolkit.

Back in the day, when I was growing up, almost everyone was puffing away on cigarettes. Now, where are all those *"good"* smokers? Well, they've all left this world. Me? I kicked that smoking habit over two decades ago, and thank goodness for that.

The oilfield business, let me tell you, had a real love affair with drinking. I joined the party a bit too much and ended up facing the beast called prostate cancer. Now, the funny thing is, I didn't listen to my own advice. It happens to the best of us, doesn't it, eh?

Here's the golden rule, though: everything in moderation.

And sometimes, you'll find yourself reminding yourself of that your whole life. Those vices can tangle you up if you let them run wild. But never, ever give up. Your family is counting on you. And, after all, family is where happiness lies. The ultimate nirvana.

You see, I've discovered that I'm a pretty tough nut to crack. I survived the trucking business for a solid three decades. Plus, I kicked prostate cancer square in the teeth. And remember that plane crash I mentioned earlier?

Well, I should've been a goner, but here I am, still kicking, and my daughter's right here with me.

So, why do you keep going? Because you've got a family to look after. It's a commitment that lasts a lifetime. You don't need to be there every single minute of the day, but when they need you, you better believe you've got to be there.

Just look at my parents; they're still at it, setting the example.

Too Fast Old and Too Slow Smart

More than four decades have passed since I first crossed paths with Walter Kapp. Back then, he was a seasoned veteran of the oil patch, while I was just a young and inexperienced fellow. I had the energy and determination, and it caught his attention. Walter decided to lend me a helping hand, and the words he shared with me that day are etched in my memory forever.

He looked at me and said, *"Bruce, I was too fast, old, and too slow smart..."* It might sound a tad cryptic initially, but let me break it down for you. What Walter was getting at is that in the race of life, there are times when we rush ahead without really thinking, and by the time we gain the wisdom we need, we've slowed down a bit.

Now, that's a lesson that's worth its weight in gold. It's a reminder that you should keep pushing forward and never, ever throw in the towel. You see, you can't go it alone on this journey. You're going to need a helping hand, and the key to that is being a good listener. The less you talk and the more you absorb from those around you, the better off you'll be.

Life, my friend, zips by at a pace that'll make your head spin. You have to keep moving forward, make use of the wisdom of those who've walked the path before you, and never, ever lose that determination to succeed.

Change of Direction

Change, my friends, it is the only thing that's as certain as the sunrise. It dances into our lives in small, everyday moments and in grand, life-altering events. And trust me, each one of us has had our share of encounters with change, both the good and the not-so-good.

Think about it for a moment. I'm pretty sure you can pull up a handful of instances from your memory where change waltzed in, unannounced and unexpected.

Sometimes, it's just a tiny blip on the radar. Like your business client suddenly cancels a meeting, leaving you with an unexpectedly free schedule. Now, you can either sit idle or seize the moment, make extra sales calls, rope in new customers, and watch your commission climb.

And then, my friends, there are those moments when change takes center stage, impacting every facet of your life. Imagine a family member, someone dear, suddenly needs more of your time due to an illness. Life flips on its head, and you find yourself juggling responsibilities you never imagined.

So here's the deal: change, whether you're hugging it like a long-lost friend or wrestling it like an unruly beast, is inevitable. It's the one constant in this rollercoaster ride we call life. But the truth is, it's not change itself that defines us; it's how we choose to adapt to it that shapes our lives.

Change often shows up unannounced, and we might instinctively treat it like an unwelcome guest. But guess what? When we welcome it with open arms, a world of positive possibilities unfolds.

Here's how:

Growth in Every Nook and Cranny

Change has this quirky habit of nudging us out of our cozy comfort zones. It might not feel like it at the time, but trust me, that's where the magic happens. When we're forced to adapt and learn new things, we stumble upon hidden capabilities, skills, and expertise we never knew we had.

Flexibility and Adaptability Rule

Comfort is comfy, no doubt. But it can also turn us into creatures of habit, resistant to anything that rocks our boat. When we open to change, we become nimble acrobats, ready to flip into new circumstances, tackle fresh situations, and connect with different people.

YES Means YES,

A Check on Your Beliefs

We all carry around a bag of beliefs, opinions, and ideas that define our worldview. It's like our own little reality bubble. When you embrace change, you start poking holes in that bubble. Meeting people with opposing views or having experiences that challenge your beliefs can lead to a shift in your perspective. It might even spark a reassessment of your life and career, reinforcing your decisions or propelling you toward loftier goals.

Unleash the Inner Beast

Change throws the spotlight on our strengths. It's like a grand unveiling of what you're truly made of. How you react when life tosses curveballs reveals the strength, courage, and determination you possess deep within.

Learning and Failing

The comfort zone is a cozy cocoon, but nothing much grows there. It's in those moments of change-induced discomfort and even failure that we learn life's most profound lessons. Think of it as a crash course in the school of life. The more we accept change, the more we learn, not just about the world but also about ourselves.

The Confidence Booster

Change is like a personal trainer for your confidence. Each time you tackle a new challenge, overcome the uncertainty, and push past your comfort zone, your confidence grows. It's like climbing a ladder – one rung at a time, your confidence builds until you're ready to reach for the stars.

I recently caught Arnold Schwarzenegger's latest documentary on Netflix, and let me tell you, it's quite the watch. I'd highly recommend giving it a go. Arnold is one remarkable individual, no doubt about it. He's also gearing up to release a new book, and I've got a feeling it's going to be a smashing

105

success. Not only will it be amazing, but it's going to make a positive impact on countless lives.

Now, when it comes to those big movie stars, they often boast about doing their own stunts, and rightfully so, they get paid handsomely for it. But let me tell you, my own life's stunts have been far more daring, and I didn't earn a dime for them. Yep, I'm talking about surviving that plane crash. That's one heck of a stunt, let me tell you.

In our journey through life, we all eventually settle in a certain direction. We find our vision, our goals, our ambitions, and our profession, and that becomes our path. But here's the thing: major events will crop up, like forks in the road, causing a change in direction. These moments are rare, perhaps happening only a few times in your entire life, maybe just three.

Take Arnold Schwarzenegger, for instance. He's had two significant shifts in his life's course. First, he was a bodybuilder and actor, entertaining the masses. Then, he took a sharp turn, becoming deeply involved in helping millions of people. That shift led him to become the governor of California, support the Special Olympics, and assist people in living better lives. And guess what? He's still on that incredible path today. From my vantage point, he's had two major direction changes.

As for me, well, I've had my fair share, three to be exact, over a span of 30 years. Initially, I was locked in one direction, working alongside my brothers and my dad. My focus was laser-sharp. But then, the time came when we decided to uproot and move to Victoria, leaving the business behind. My brother had a rather blunt chat with me one day and basically said, *"If you're going to pretend to work, I'll pretend to pay you."*

Fair enough, right?

So, we packed our bags and made the move. If we'd stayed put in Calgary, I'd still be cruising along in that same direction.

Our lives took an unexpected turn when, just a year after arriving in Victoria, my beloved wife Charlene received a devastating diagnosis of breast cancer. It was a heart-wrenching 10-month battle, and she ultimately passed away. That's when my life's direction shifted once more.

Now, let me tell you, I've never been one to throw in the towel, but these trials pushed me to the limits and then some. I had a mantra playing on repeat in my head:

"You can't give up; your family needs you now more than ever."

I remember talking to my brother Kevin during this time. I told him, "I'm going to write a book." He asked, "What are you going to call it? 'I've Had Enough'?" But no, I had a different title in mind, something that echoed in my heart: *"Yes means yes, and everything else means no."* He nodded in agreement, and that's how the title came to be.

You see, a multitude of people stepped up to support me during this trying period, and I'm eternally grateful for their kindness. These are the moments that have shaped my life, and the lessons I've learned, I've distilled into simple wisdom.

Now, I don't have a fancy degree to my name; my education was more about street smarts than book smarts. But I have this burning desire to share my experiences, my emotions, and the things that truly mattered in my life. Perhaps, in some way, they might matter to you, too.

I've always strived to give my best, no matter the circumstances. Anyone who knows me can vouch for one thing: *I never, ever give up.*

Chapter 9

Being Present

"You need to be in team sports, not just in school."

You know, the technology we've got these days is downright impressive. It's like a whirlwind of innovation that's sweeping across the world and changing everything in its path. I mean, think about it: folks like Steve Jobs have redefined the game. They've taken the world and given it a good shake. It's like they're saying, *"Hey, let's switch things up a bit!"*

And you know what?

It's not just the tech giants who are riding this wave. Even Warren Buffett, the sage of investing, has hopped on the tech train. He used to say he'd steer clear of tech because it was like trying to understand rocket science in Swahili, but now he's all about it. He's got a soft spot for Apple, and who can blame him?

Warren didn't want to be that guy who's stuck in the past, clinging to outdated ways like buying a thousand horses when Henry Ford's cruisin' by in a car. Nope, he's a smart cookie, and he knows that embracing change is the name of the game.

Let me tell you a secret about the tech world. It's a double-edged sword, my friends. A blessing and a curse. Remember when I talked about being in team sports and not just in school? Well, it's like that with technology, too.

You see, I'm sure you've noticed this — pull up to an intersection, and you'll see folks strolling across the street, heads buried in their phones. They don't even know if it's a *"walk"* or *"don't walk"* sign. Walk into a restaurant, and there's a couple, both glued to their screens. Are they texting each other? Who knows?

Now, don't get me wrong, we're all guilty of it, including yours truly. Technology is a bit like a war zone; you can block, like, or unblock people and give them thumbs up or down, all in the blink of an eye. Sometimes, we react so fast that we don't even have time to think.

But here's where I'm a tad concerned, especially when it comes to the younger generation. When you hand a young one a phone, how do you control what they see? How can you guide them to make the right choices? Back in the day, when we got in trouble, they took our phones away.

But now, with all this technology and AI (that's artificial intelligence, by the way), it's like they want to do the thinking for you. They're bombarding young minds with content and subtly making decisions for them. It's a bit of a scare, to be honest. We could end up with a whole generation that doesn't think for itself. They call them *"followers"* for a reason, you know?

These tech giants they're enormous, and they've got influence that can rival a tidal wave. Sometimes, it feels like we're stuck in a *"take it or leave it"* situation. But hey, we'll figure it out. We always do.

You can't bring the same tools to the same problem

Alright, so what's our game plan here?

Let's be real; none of us have all the answers, but we're all in this boat together, and we've got to navigate these tech waters.

You know, if you stroll into a store today and hand someone a fifty-dollar bill, it's like you've handed them a piece of ancient treasure. They look at it like, *"What do I do with this relic? Do I need to find change from the Stone Age?"* It's bizarre how some places don't even want to touch our cash anymore.

Now, let's talk about our youngsters and their shiny new phones. It's absolutely vital that we set those gadgets upright, especially if they're under 18. One tip: make sure they chip in for the phone bill. Remember that saying, *"Cash is king"*? It still holds true.

And here's a piece of advice: be there for your kids. Listen to them. Otherwise, they'll scurry off to their rooms, glued to those screens. There are so many platforms these days; some I haven't even heard of, and new ones keep popping up.

Now, some smart moms and dads out there have found success. They don't just hand over phones like candy; they make their kids earn them. No phones at night, and you should follow suit. Keep an eye on your screen time; it's a sneaky thing. Also, check if your schools allow phones in class; they really shouldn't. Lockers are the place for them. Oh, and don't even think about bringing phones to the dinner table. Back in my day, TV was off-limits, and that was when we only had two channels. Phones during a meal or a gathering? That's just plain rude and shows a lack of respect.

When I snagged my first iPhone, dropping it in water was a death sentence. Now, you can fish it out of the pool, and it's like, *"Water? What water?"* Steve Jobs said, *"We build products people don't even know they want yet,"* and boy, did he change the world. But now, it's our turn to adapt and make this tech work for us.

See, back in the day, folks said people didn't communicate enough. We had those phone booths, and you had to rustle up change from your pocket. Nowadays, finding a phone booth is like spotting a unicorn, and who carries coins anymore?

Yet, here we are with all this fancy tech, and some say we still don't communicate properly. You flip through news channels, and it's like they're speaking different languages. But you know what? Technology didn't solve everything.

Sure, tech can make you feel more secluded. It's got me pondering the days when you could buy or sell a house with a simple handshake, not a bunch of digital signatures. But here's the kicker: in every relationship, be it business or personal, they all say the same thing — *communication is the big kahuna.*

You know, there's this great quote from Garth Brooks, and it's wisdom worth cherishing. He said, *"Technology can be a blessing or a curse,"* and boy, is he on the money with that one.

Sending pictures to your loved ones and dear friends, it's like magic. There's a world of benefits wrapped up in technology, and that's what we need to keep talking about. We've got to sing the praises of tech's good side because, let's face it, people only change when they really want to or when they absolutely have to.

And here's the deal: I don't see folks changing their tech-loving ways anytime soon. They're head over heels for their gadgets, and that's not changing overnight. It's a bit of a conundrum, isn't it?

I find myself saying the same thing over and over again, but it's worth repeating. Do your best to make those decisions based on your own knowledge and experience. That's the best advice I can dish out. Welcome the good that tech brings, but keep an eye out for those potential pitfalls.

The Power of Face To Face Communication

The incredible power of face-to-face communication has always fascinated me. I think of it like this secret weapon that can supercharge our interactions, whether it's with colleagues we've known for years or potential business partners, we're just getting to know.

Research shows that when we meet face-to-face, our requests are a whopping 34 times more effective than sending an email. That's right, folks! There's some real magic in that physical presence. Even a simple handshake can work wonders, boosting cooperation and improving negotiation outcomes.

MIT's Human Dynamics Lab did some cool stuff, too. They tracked performance in various industries and found that the most valuable communication happens in person. In fact, around 35 percent of a team's performance can be explained by how often they chat face-to-face. *That's some impressive math!*

But it's not just data that tells this story; anecdotes are pretty convincing, too. Experts in organizational behavior say that face-to-face meetings capture a person's full attention. They cut through the clutter of multitasking and let us focus on the important stuff.

René Siegel, a professor and CEO, puts it perfectly: "We're all in the people business, no matter our industry. And there's a difference between business chit-chat and those deep, meaningful business relationships. The latter only happens when we spend time talking about stuff that truly matters to us."

So, what's the lesson here?

Well, not all meetings are created equal. That's where planners and venues come into play. They help create the magic by curating experiences that go beyond the norm. Hilton, for example, is all about adding a dash of wellness and sustainability to their meetings. They're turning traditional gatherings into experiences that leave a mark, like their *"Yoga and Yogurt"* package or the *"Cut & Create"* salad adventure.

Hilton, being the global hospitality leader it is, can help you orchestrate these memorable gatherings in the world's most fabulous destinations. They've got properties all over and a dedicated team that's all about making your events welcoming and engaging.

Now, with all the pandemic-induced virtual craziness, it might seem like face-to-face is taking a back seat. But don't be fooled! Even in this brave new world, where virtual meetings are the norm, we'll still crave that in-person magic.

Why, you ask?

Because there are four pillars of management development-collaboration, innovation, acculturation, and dedication that need that face-to-face kickstart. They thrive on real, physical interaction.

Collaboration is all about building trust and understanding. Innovation needs the sparks that fly when creative minds meet. Acculturation, well, that's about creating a shared culture. And dedication? That's about feeling like you're part of something bigger.

But how do you create these awesome in-person experiences?

It's all about these *"design drivers."*

Purposeful focus

When you're together, it's hard to get distracted. You're fully in the moment, and that helps you concentrate better. Imagine creating an offsite experience for your team, where they're away from the daily grind and can really focus.

Interpersonal bonding

Trust and support are key to collaboration and innovation. So, encourage your team to open up and get to know each other personally. It's like building a big, happy work family.

Deep learning

Learning isn't just about knowing facts; it's about understanding and applying them in real life. That happens best when you're in a group, sharing experiences and insights.

Unencumbered experimentation

Trying out new ideas is tough when you're worried about stepping on toes. But face-to-face time builds trust, and trust is perfect for free-flowing experimentation.

Structured serendipity

Sometimes, the best stuff happens when you least expect it. So, create opportunities for chance encounters and informal chats. You never know what brilliant ideas might pop up!

I know what you're thinking. With all these virtual tools, why bother with face-to-face?

Well, because there's something irreplaceable about being in the same room. It's about those human moments that no Zoom call can replicate.

Sure, we've come a long way in terms of tech, but nothing beats a heart-to-heart conversation. It's time to embrace the magic of face-to-face interaction. So, next time, you need to make a real connection, ditch the emails and meetings, and go meet someone for real. Your relationships—and your business—will thank you for it.

The COVID-19 pandemic ushered in surprising changes in our lives, and one of the most significant shifts was the way we interacted with our screens. Research from 2021 revealed that in 2020, young people spent an average of 28.5 hours per week on their phones. That's a jump from 25.9 hours just two years prior. For many adults, screen time also soared during the pandemic, with estimates suggesting a 60-80% increase.

Now, let's dive into the real deal — how does all this screen time affect us, especially the older adults?

Well, the impact isn't all sunshine and rainbows. Excessive screen time has been linked to a host of problems. It's not just a case of digital eye strain (although that's very real), but also poor sleep and a negative hit to our mental well-being. Depression and anxiety rates have been climbing, and it's no coincidence that our screen time has been soaring, too.

But hey, before you start counting the minutes you spend on your phone and spiral into panic mode, let's remember one simple fact: *it's not just about the quantity of time spent. It's about the quality of what you're doing.*

Dr. Yalda T. Uhls, a psychology professor at UCLA, points out that the content you're consuming matters as much as the clock ticking away. Binge-watching a Netflix documentary isn't the same as mindlessly scrolling through Instagram.

So, what should you do if your phone report shows a scary number?

Dr. Dimitri Christakis, a pediatrician and screen time researcher, suggests a different approach. Don't just worry about the grand total; think about how you spent that time. Social media apps often get the side-eye here because they tend to be the most concerning.

Here's a five-question reality check Dr. Uhls recommends: *Are you sleeping well? Eating well? Socializing and leaving the house? Is work on track? Are you getting some exercise?*

If you tick these boxes, don't sweat it too much.

However, we do need some guidelines. Here are a few to ponder:

Limit social media

Stick to 30-60 minutes a day for better mental health. Remember the study about college students who limited themselves to 30 minutes of social media a day? Their symptoms of depression and loneliness actually decreased.

Spend screen-free time

Aim for at least three to four hours a day without screens. That means disconnecting from the digital world and reconnecting with the real one. It's not just about limiting screen time; it's about expanding other, healthier activities.

Ditch screens before bedtime

Using screens right before bedtime can wreck your sleep quality. Try to give your eyes a break for at least an hour before hitting the sack.

Take eye breaks

To protect your eyes from digital eye strain, adopt the 20-20-20 rule. For every 20 minutes of screen time, take a 20-second break and focus on something 20 feet away. Your eyes will thank you.

Parent by example

If you're a parent, your screen time habits influence your kids. Set boundaries and model good behavior.

Manage your news consumption

Constant news updates can lead to anxiety. Set specific times to check the news, and follow trusted sources to avoid falling into the doomscrolling trap.

Curate your social media feeds

Unfollow or mute accounts that bring you down. Your mental health is more important than worrying about someone's feelings.

Turn off notifications

Do you really need to know about every like, comment, or email immediately? Keep essential notifications on, and silence the rest.

Maintain your focus

Use one screen for one task. Don't let your attention hop around multiple devices simultaneously.

Resist screen time when bored or stressed

Ask yourself if screen time is the best way to alleviate boredom or stress. Sometimes, a walk or meditation can be more effective.

No screens during meals

Make mealtime a screen-free zone, whether you're eating alone or with others.

Be present with others

When spending time with friends or family, put your phone aside and engage fully in the moment.

Designate screen-free times

Set periods during the day when screens are off-limits, giving you more free time for other activities.

Create screen-free zones

Make certain areas of your home, like your bedroom, screen-free zones to promote relaxation and better sleep.

Seek alternatives

Replace screen time with other fulfilling activities that you genuinely enjoy. Even just a few minutes can make a big difference.

See, it's not about eradicating screens from your life; it's about finding a balanced, healthy relationship with them. Screens are part of our modern world, but with some thoughtful strategies, you can take control and make your screen time work for you, not against you.

"Be present in your own life."

Learning to be more present can truly transform your life. Trust me, this a skill that can enrich your life in countless ways.

So, you're sitting on your cozy couch, savoring a bowl of popcorn while engrossed in a movie, aimlessly scrolling through Instagram, and half-heartedly listening to your partner recount their day. In the middle of this chaos, your mind is preoccupied with a task scheduled for next week. Later, as you lie in bed, you realize you didn't fully enjoy the movie, your popcorn tasted bland, and your partner's words fell on deaf ears. Worse yet, you're far from relaxed or rejuvenated.

In our fast-paced lives, distractions surround us, making it increasingly challenging to focus on just one thing at a time. Stress, anxiety, and the weight of regrets further impede our ability to relish the present. But residing in the moment, though demanding, can be a game-changer for your relationships, productivity, and, most significantly, your overall well-being.

Living in the moment is about embracing the here and now. Instead of letting your thoughts wander, you channel your attention toward your current actions, sensations, and surroundings.

Now, let's explore some invaluable tips to help you master the art of being present:

Monotasking

In a world that glorifies multitasking, monotasking shines as a secret superpower. While multitasking can be inevitable, it pays to be mindful about how we approach it. Research suggests that juggling tasks can hinder focus, emotional regulation, and memory. Multitasking may seem efficient, but it scatters your attention. Instead, channel your focus into one task. It may feel overwhelming at first, but it pays off in increased productivity and a heightened sense of presence. Try monotasking, focusing on one task at a time. This practice enhances your presence and attentiveness, particularly during studying or work.

Breathing Exercises

Don't underestimate the magic of mindful breathing. It's a potent tool for managing emotions, nurturing mental wellness, and anchoring yourself in the present. Concentrate on the sensations of inhaling and exhaling, the soothing sound of your breath, and your body's response to it. These simple breathwork techniques can cultivate awareness of your bodily sensations. Deep breathing can calm your mind and maintain focus. Try techniques like the 4-7-8 breathing method to center yourself in the present.

Meditation

Meditation is the quintessential path to living in the moment. It's a practice that brings presence in your body and mind. Whether you choose to sit quietly in a serene space with your eyes closed or rely on meditation apps like Headspace and Calm for guidance, the key is to let thoughts come and go while focusing on your breath. With time, meditation becomes an invaluable habit.

Mindfulness-Based Stress Reduction (MBSR)

For those seeking to elevate their mindfulness practice, consider MBSR. Developed by Jon Kabat—Zinn in 1979, this program melds traditional Buddhist mindfulness and meditation practices.

Mindful Movement

Exercise often beckons us to pause, connect with our bodies, and tune into our breath. Engaging in mindful movement brings you closer to the present moment. Yoga, tai chi, qigong, and pilates are prime examples, but even a leisurely, mindful walk can work wonders. Redirect your focus from to-do lists or worries to your breath, posture, and surroundings. Physical activity encourages mindfulness by connecting you to your body and breathing.

Reducing Distractions

Distractions, though sometimes helpful, can disrupt your ability to stay present. Identify and mitigate these distractions. If your favorite podcast hinders breakfast enjoyment, opt for a silent morning meal. When reviewing your day with a loved one, placing your phone out of reach can curb the temptation to check it. Constantly checking your devices can pull you away from the present. Set aside time each day to disconnect from screens and reconnect with your surroundings.

Journaling

Writing is a therapeutic way to engage with your thoughts. Journaling, especially free writing (where thoughts flow freely onto the page), trains you to slow down your thoughts and pay more attention to them. Alternatively, journal prompts can serve as a structured entry point into your own mind.

Notice Your Surroundings

Take moments throughout your day to truly observe your environment. *What do you see on the walls, floor, or ceiling? How many windows surround you?* This simple exercise can ground you in the present.

Practice Gratitude

Be grateful for what you have right now rather than fixating on what's lacking. Daily lists of things you're grateful for can shift your perspective and keep you rooted in the present.

Show Acceptance

Accept things as they are rather than how you wish them to be. Recognize that not everything is within your control, and practice acceptance to let go of undue stress.

Seek Positive Social Support

Surrounding yourself with supportive, positive individuals makes it easier to remain present and creates a happier, more fulfilling life.

Be Mindful of Everything You Do

Whether eating a meal or scrolling through your phone, engage fully in the activity at hand. Pay attention to your senses and the world around you to bring more awareness into your life.

Now, why is this all so essential?

Living in the moment equips you to savor life's pleasures, connect deeply with loved ones, and immerse yourself fully in tasks or leisure activities. It soothes racing thoughts, taming the beast of overthinking and anxiety.

Many of us often find ourselves dwelling on the past or fretting about the future. These tendencies rob us of the joy found in the present. The good news is that learning to be more mindful and live in the moment can infuse your life with greater appreciation, reduce stress, and quell anxiety.

In essence, living in the moment means giving your full attention to what's happening right now without being entangled in past regrets or future anxieties. It's a skill worth mastering, one that leads to a more balanced, joyful, and fulfilled life. Let me leave you with this one final food for thought,

"All you have is this moment. Don't let it slip away."

Chapter 10

Conclusion

As we come to the end of our time together, let's recall the lessons we have learned so far.

"Yes Means Yes"

Let me reiterate this simple phrase that can change your life. *"Yes means yes; everything else means no."* It's not just a string of words; it's a profound concept that I stumbled upon through a conversation with my older brother, Murray. You see, Murray was a man of few words, but those words were like gold. He believed in clear, written requirements to get things done right. I admired his no-nonsense approach, and I want you to make it your life mantra.

Starting Your Day Right

Now, we discussed how this philosophy can revolutionize your daily life. It all begins with how you kickstart your day. Your morning routine can actually set the tone for everything that follows. If we just focus on practical morning habits, they can make a world of difference. From gratitude journaling to the simple act of making your bed, these small changes can infuse your day with positivity and purpose.

Welcoming Life's Lessons

Life's full of surprises, and yes, mistakes happen. I urged you to acknowledge the inevitable bumps in the road and, more importantly, learn from them. At that time, my daughter and I survived a plane crash. Despite all the checks and precautions, a mistake happened. But here's the lesson: *mistakes aren't the end; they're the beginning of something new.*

The Currency of Trust

We learned that trust is the foundation of all meaningful relationships. We also talked about how it is essential in both personal and professional spheres. The highlight was when you learned how you can build and nurture trust because, my friend, trust is what makes the world go 'round.

Are You a Leader or a Follower?

I asked you to self-reflect and ask yourselves if you are a leader or follower and get to know yourselves better. We explored the qualities that distinguish leaders from followers and why developing your leadership skills matters. Remember, It's not about titles; it's about making a difference, and we explored the practical skills that can empower you to do just that.

Seizing the Value of Time

Time is the most precious currency we have, more valuable than gold. We talked about making every second count. We learned how to maximize your time, from avoiding procrastination to sidestepping distractions. I offered you some practical tips to help you invest your time wisely.

Embracing Lifelong Learning

Learning isn't confined to the classroom; it's a lifelong journey. This is when we delved into the concept of continuous learning, drawing from personal experiences like the loss of my wife to cancer. Life throws curveballs, and we learned how learning to adapt is the key to thriving.

Unyielding Perseverance

When life gets tough, the tough get going. We celebrated the indomitable spirit of determination. It's not about giving in; it's about never giving up. I shared some personal challenges and triumphs, and we investigated why persistence is your most potent weapon.

Rediscovering Presence

In our smartphone-saturated world, it's easy to lose sight of what truly matters. I helped you rediscover the joy of genuine human connection, moving beyond the digital distractions. We discussed the perils of smartphone addiction, and I provided practical tips to be more present in your life.

Two Key Takeaways: First, the power of teamwork in both business and personal life. Second, when life delivers its blows, don't let your loved ones who you love you live your tragedies.

Let me tell you, my friend, these two lessons have been like guiding stars in my journey. The first is the incredible strength of collaborating with a trusted team, whether in the professional world or in your personal circles. And the second, the ultimate truth — when tragedy knocks on your door, don't let your loved ones carry the weight of your pain. They don't deserve it.

Penning down this book has been a cathartic experience for me. My hope is it does the same for you.

So, there you have it, my friend. My parting words to you are simple: repeat this phrase to yourself daily, *"Yes means yes, everything else means no."* and watch your life transform for the best! You've got this!

Printed in the USA
CPSIA information can be obtained
at www.ICGtesting.com
LVHW052129250424
778511LV00008B/41